.Marian
Bak
Mus

D1320603

BFI Modern Classics

Rob White
Series Editor

BFI Modern Classics is a series of critical studies of films produced over the last three decades. An array of writers explore their chosen films, offering a range of perspectives on the dominant art and entertainment medium in contemporary culture. The series gathers together snapshots of our passion for and understanding of recent movies.

Hanson directs Basinger

L.A. Confidential

Manohla Dargis

bfi Publishing

First published in 2003 by the
British Film Institute
21 Stephen Street, London W1T 1LN

The British Film Institute promotes greater
understanding and appreciation of,
and access to, film and moving image
culture in the UK.

British Library Cataloguing-in-Publication Data
A catalogue record for this book is available
from the British Library

ISBN 0-85170-944-3

Series design by Andrew Barron &
Collis Clements Associates

Typeset in Italian Garamond and Swiss 721BT
by D R Bungay Associates, Burghfield, Berks

Printed in Great Britain by
Cromwell Press, Trowbridge, Wiltshire

Contents

Acknowledgments

I would like to thank James Ellroy, Jeannine Oppewall and especially Curtis Hanson for being so generous with their time. Thanks also go to Helen Knode, Amy Taubin, Nick James and F.X. Feeney, all of whom helped along the way; to my editor, Rob White, whose patience and intelligence were unstinting; and, finally, to Lou Amdur, always my first and best reader.

Crowe, Hanson, Rifkin and Pearce on set

Introduction: A Bright, Guilty City

Here America will build its great city of the Pacific, the most fantastic city in the world.
Carey McWilliams on Los Angeles, 1946

Is the City of Angeles Going to Hell?
Time magazine, 1993

The trouble begins with the sun, that spotlight which floods the city, throwing everything into relief. The sun and all it suggests, the infinite pleasures and permanent tans, is how the world knows Los Angeles, one of the few instantly recognisable modern metropolises without a defining architectural totem – save for the Hollywood sign, of course. The world knows Los Angeles through the movies and television, and if you live here long enough, you realise it's not much different for some Angelenos. It is the city's defining paradox that even as it has become one of a handful of global cities in the last half-century, it remains principally identified with its fantasy industries. In his film *The Lady from Shanghai*, the sailor played by Orson Welles gets off a boat in Acapulco, squints at the sun and declares, 'It's a bright, guilty world.' It's easy to imagine that Welles was thinking of Los Angeles when he said that line, for it neatly captures the popular view of the city as transparent and opaque at once, a dreamscape of seduction and shame. Welles's path to and from L.A. is familiar, but it's worth noting that he never could stay away for long. Whether out of habit or necessity, this city of bright and fallen angels keeps a tight hold on those who loathe it; perhaps especially to those who do.

When native son James Ellroy published *L.A. Confidential* in 1990, Los Angeles was in the midst of a plague season that transformed it from an ambivalent dreamscape into a national fixation, at once the talk-show host's late-night joke and the new urban theorist's reigning cautionary tale. (Ellroy skipped town permanently in 1981.) For nine seemingly interminable years beginning in the late 1980s, the city suffered drought, devastating fires, a fatal earthquake, torrential floods, mud-slides – along with one of the worst civil disturbances in United States history – that remade it into the very noir landscape the movies had production-designed for decades. When the film of Ellroy's novel was released into theatres in 1997, the worst of the city's recent miseries seemed to be over, or maybe that's what those of us who live here liked to tell ourselves. The fires and floods had subsided, as had the civil unrest. The problems persisted but the streets were again clear for production. Once more, the movie-makers could take possession of Los Angeles; they could wrench it from the headlines and return it to the screen, where to all appearances it belonged.

Los Angeles is, after all, one of Hollywood's bad habits – or is it the other way around? Just as the movies can't seem to leave the city alone, it is impossible to envision L.A. outside a film frame, so often has its sprawl, its night, its downtown been beamed across the world. What was there left to say about L.A. that the movies hadn't already told us? In the age of the blockbuster, what was left of the movies themselves? For Curtis Hanson,

Hanson with Spacey

the director *L.A. Confidential*, and his co-writer, Brian Helgeland, the answer was: plenty. Closely based on Ellroy's book, their film redefines the city by embracing everything that the real Los Angeles historically, at times murderously, tried to hide. Set in the early 1950s, the Good Old Days of our collective imagination – which, for many, looks a lot like the golden age of Hollywood – it is a period piece that speaks to the city's recent hard times even as it conceives of a Los Angeles that is more than the sum of its disasters. With its patina of glamour and hard-boiled interior, it is a period film that looks as if it could have been produced in 1950s Hollywood if studio self-censorship hadn't gotten in the way of all the sex and the sadism, the institutional racism and government corruption. A period piece that follows the contours (if not the conventions) of the classical studio system and, at the same time, critiques that system by exposing everything the movies once refused to reveal.

As Ellroy had done before him, Hanson resurrected the Los Angeles of his childhood with *L.A. Confidential*. For both men, the resurrection was an act of nostalgia for a lost city and a lost time, but it was also a way of revisiting their respective obsessions: Ellroy's for the city and its crimes, Hanson's for the city and its movies. That these twinned obsessions could dovetail in one masterfully wrought Hollywood movie seems ironic given the state of the art during the 1990s. In the mid-1990s, movie-making in the United States was increasingly divided between low-budget independent film driven by vision and high-concept studio movies driven by box office. Free-floating above this divide were designated auteurs who roamed from studio to studio looking for patronage. For a film-maker like Hanson, who had been born during the studios' golden age and come of creative age during the New Hollywood movement, and held to the promise of both eras that cinema aspire to the condition of art, 1990s Hollywood seemed an unlikely home. That it was such a home was a minor miracle, a flicker of hope in a place where art had been all but eclipsed by industry. In this sense, *L.A. Confidential* is not just a movie but a dream of the movies – how they once were and how they could be again. This, then, is a Los Angeles movie – this time with the lights turned on.

1 Watching the Detectives

It begins with a blare of horns – of saxophones, not automobiles as you might expect of a film set in the car-culture capital of the world – and the relentlessly cheerful dictate 'to accentuate the positive'. Taken from Johnny Mercer's arrangement of his and Harold Arlen's 1944 wartime hit, 'Ac-cent-tchu-ate the Positive', the words ring out over the first image in *L.A. Confidential*, a stack of postcards, one of which bears the legend spelled out in big, bold type: 'Greetings From Los Angeles, California'. In 1952, the year that the film opens, it was the sort of postcard a tourist might have mailed to the folks back home for a glimpse of palm trees and a stretch of beach, along with a bird's-eye view of the city's totemic city hall – scenes from a world of endless sunshine. Here, though, the postcard serves as a visitor's pass both to Lost Los Angeles and to the film itself, a reassuring, gently sentimental point of entry for the extended montage which it launches. 'Come to Los Angeles,' exhorts an unseen male narrator. 'The sun shines bright. The beaches are wide and inviting and the orange groves stretch as far as the eye can see.'

The voice belongs to Sid Hudgens (played by Danny DeVito), the resident scam artist for a scandal magazine called *Hush-Hush*. Hudgens will prove to be a linchpin in the story to come, right now, though, heard but not yet seen, he is a tour guide cum sideshow carny for an excursion into the city's past, real and imaginary. Onscreen, booster image follows booster image, and citrus trees give way to factory workers and 'jobs a-plenty'. There are images of sylvan fields and manicured suburban lawns on which smiling children play ball. 'Inside every house', Hudgens promises, 'a happy all-American family.' Just as the vision of everyday Angeleno bliss reaches its apex, the city's iconography is abrupt subsumed by that of Hollywood: Marilyn Monroe and Jane Russell beam their brights in front of a bulwark of waving fans. Frank Sinatra squires Deborah Kerr at one of those convergences of idols and idolatry known as The Movie Premiere. The hucksterism in Sid's voice curves around a menacing bend. 'It's paradise on earth,' he pledges, right before releasing a cascade of laughter, the rat-a-tat of sunshine cynicism. 'That's what they tell ya anyway. Because they're selling an image, they're selling it through movies, radio and television.'

Hollywood has been eclipsing Los Angeles virtually from the moment the latter swallowed the former. The small community of Hollywood incorporated in 1903; seven years later Los Angeles, which had been keeping its landlocked neighbour strategically dry, absorbed the water-thirsty burg of several thousand. It was around this same time that movie people started pouring in from the East, staking claims on the area to take advantage of the climate, variegated terrain and the distance from the patents office on the other coast. In 1909, actor-turned-director Francis Boggs set up shop behind a Chinese laundry on downtown's Olive Street (thirty years later, novelist John Fante walked down Olive, then fallen on hard times, and wrote of houses 'reeking with murder stories'[1]). The following year, writer and director D. W. Griffith arrived with over two dozen movie colonists in tow. By the end of 1911, when the Nestor Company had built the area's first movie studio on the northwest corner of Gower Street and Sunset Boulevard, the histories of Los Angeles and Hollywood were twinned for good.

From the 1910s on, Hollywood would become a Mecca for American hopefuls (the Algonquin roundtable, Ben Hecht, countless more) and for habitués and refugees from Luis Buñuel, Sergei Eisenstein and Bertolt Brecht to Billy Wilder, Fritz Lang and Douglas Sirk. As the movies reached out to the rest of the country, seducing new audiences with each passing decade, the rest of the country reached out to Los Angeles, entranced by the area's self-professed plenty as well as its actual potential. The nation's dream of the city, dazzling and over-baked, would eventually transform Los Angeles into a kind of eternal frontier – the last pit stop for the American dream itself. It was a covenant that would inspire countless movies, popular songs and, later, television programmes, along with an indigenous literary tradition that was by turns idealistic and cynical. Yet while some sang the city's praises or at least invoked its promise ('Los Angeles, give me some of you,' entreats Fante in his 1939 bohemian classic, *Ask the Dust*), it was the bitter, at times dystopian, voices that often sounded the loudest, from Nathanael West's Depression-era

dirge, *The Day of the Locust*, to Ellroy's self-anointed 'L.A. Quartet', published some fifty years later.[2]

The third novel in the quartet, *L.A. Confidential*, begins in early 1950 and winds through a decade that saw Los Angeles begin to shake off its identity as a rough-and-tumble backwater to become the fastest-growing metropolis in the nation. Hanson's movie compresses the novel's eight years into a few taut weeks, beginning on Christmas Eve night, 1952. Despite the condensation, which whittled down the original book's 496 pages to 130 screenplay pages, with entire subplots and characters excised, the story's backdrop remains the same, that of a city in the throes of violent transformation. There are gangland murders, corrupt police and politicians, prostitute and pornography rings, race riots as well as the quieter, insidious violence of institutionalised racism, the slander industry and the lingering tremors of anti-Communist hysteria – some of it hinted

Los Angeles – from paradise to sprawl

at during the opening credit montage. This seamless mixture of found footage and photographs selected by Hanson himself serves as the film's opening credit sequence, but more instructively functions as something of a narrative road map, a guide on how to watch the ensuing film.

It's to this end that when the first images of green trees, blue skies and white people flicker across the screen, they're as unthreatening (if as suspect) as a chamber of commerce promotional reel. Even before Hollywood intrudes on the scene, though, and Hudgens's voice grows suggestively mocking, scraping against the pictures, the original meaning of the images starts to shift. The seemingly neutral and uninflected are answered by the increasingly ridiculous and hyperbolic: empty fields turn into freeway construction sites, family meals mutate into fast-food living. Citrus groves are supplanted by toothy women swimming amid bobbing oranges, the 'natural' bounty transformed into a silly, vulgar public relations spectacle, some might say, as silly and vulgar as the city itself.[3] Even glamour tarnishes, as footage of Monroe and Sinatra, each of whom had ties to organised crime, is followed, in turn, by the introduction of gangster Mickey Cohen, a minor character in the film, whose dramatised arrest on tax evasion concludes the montage and launches the narrative.

Mickey Cohen busted, 1951

Here, then, is the city of dreams and city of nightmares – past, present and future – in which those in *L.A. Confidential* find, then lose, their way.

In *L.A. Confidential*, no one and nothing are what they first seem. Although the film contains a central mystery – the who and the why behind a mass murder at a coffee shop called the Nite Owl – the narrative is, in classic detective fashion, an obstacle course of ruses. Even first impressions are intentionally misleading. After the arrest of Mickey Cohen, the film cuts to a series of quick-sketch scenes that offer up a fast, telling look at the three detectives at its centre: officers Wendell 'Bud' White and Edmund Exley, and sergeant Jack 'Hollywood Jack' Vincennes (played, respectively, by Russell Crowe, Guy Pearce and Kevin Spacey). In every one of his inaugural scenes, each of these three men will be caught in a revealing moment, negotiating a critical interaction that will send shock waves through their respective lives and the events that will eventually connect them. Importantly, and because this isn't the story of God's lonely man, each will also almost immediately be shown in the company of the secondary character who will most profoundly affect – by love, by accident and by wrong – the seismic, determining shifts in their moral landscapes. These are, then, the defining moments when Bud first meets the prostitute Lynn Bracken (played by Kim Basinger), when Jack

Bud and Stens at 4216 Evergreen; 'Why don't you dance with a man for a change?'

negotiates one of his final deals with Sid Hudgens (DeVito) and when Ed makes his initial bid to outflank his superior officer, Captain Dudley Smith (played by James Cromwell).

The introductions begin with Bud, seen in close-up behind the wheel of an unmarked police car. Slouched in the back and taking pulls off a bottle sits his long-time partner, Dick ('Stens') Stensland, who, with a tight corrosive laugh, says, 'You're like Santa Claus with that list, Bud. Except everyone on it's been naughty.' It's evening and although the address Bud recites into the police radio is '4216 Evergreen', this could be any one of Los Angeles' post-war neighbourhoods, lined with modest starter homes and shrouded in quiet. Except that at 4216 Evergreen a man is roughing up a woman. As Stens keeps laughing, Bud storms the house and with a few hard tugs brings down the illuminated plastic Santa and reindeer adorning its roof. The man throws opens the front door ('Who in the hell are you?'), and the detective starts punching. After beating the man to the ground, Bud handcuffs him to the house, warning that if he touches the woman again he'll be arrested for a 'kiddie raper beef'. 'You know', says Bud, 'what they do to kiddie rapers in [San] Quentin?' He then asks the lurking woman if she has somewhere to go. She nods and heads toward the family car, adding by way of goodbye, 'Merry Christmas, huh?'

When Hanson pitched his vision of *L.A. Confidential* to producer Arnon Milchan, he used a photograph of Aldo Ray to suggest his vision of Bud. A former Navy frogman and small-town California sheriff, Ray was blond and burly, with a gravel voice and a neck as thick as a tree trunk. He made his first film in 1951 and during that decade and into the next two played a series of regular Joes for which he is best remembered. He was a finer actor than many of his assignments and every bit up to his greatest movies. Two of his best – George Cukor's 1952 melodrama *The Marrying Kind* and, at the opposite end of the genre spectrum, Anthony Mann's 1957 *Men in War*, set in a Korean battlefield – showed that Ray's gift was for characters who seemed somehow wounded by masculinity. The actor's meaty physicality, combined with a voice which often seemed on the verge of re-breaking, was a prison house of sorts, at odds with the anguished machismo of Marlon Brando and the febrile neuroses of James Stewart that defined post-war Hollywood. Yet Ray's physicality was also the citadel from which he could safely betray tender feeling as a despondent father in *The Marrying Kind* and as a protective surrogate son in *Men in War*.

Until Crowe, few Hollywood actors could embody this masculine–feminine admixture as persuasively as Ray. Born in New Zealand and raised in Australia, Crowe first came to Hanson's notice in the 1992 film *Romper Stomper*, in which he starred as a skinhead who steers a gang of neo-Nazis through the usual thuggish mindlessness and ends up a victim of his own nihilism. As he would time and again, and as Aldo Ray had done before him, the actor wore masculinity like a carapace. It was an intently physical performance, as many of Crowe's are, but what makes it archetypal wasn't the musculature that hardened his shell further, turning his body into a weapon and a shield, but the hurt he summoned up in his eyes. Lacking heartbreaking beauty and innate physical grace, Crowe has emerged as a stirring albeit unlikely creature of passion in whose expressively wet eyes you can catch sight of a mind struggling against flesh, the human in struggle with the animal, the female in struggle with the male. In *L.A. Confidential*, the actor's beefy body gives Bud a taurine physicality but the character isn't simply a bull; he is a bull seething with emotions so powerful it seems as if they could burst through his clothes.

Contemporary Hollywood had been dominated since the mid-1980s by incarnations of ironic maleness that were alternately cartoon and cool. For Hanson's adaptation of *L.A. Confidential* to work, however, there could be nothing ironic about its period re-creation, its violence or its characters. On paper, Ellroy's women and men are exaggerated, extreme to the occasional edge of satire, but they are also deadly serious, in some measure because the novelist doesn't grant them the privilege of historic hindsight. As a consequence, because they don't know any better, they say and do things that most modern authors would be too embarrassed (or politically correct) to have characters say and do – racist, vile, nasty things. Ellroy revels in uncivil society and his Bud is an unreconstructed Neanderthal who doesn't just jump off the page, he rages, making Crowe, a performer with a total commitment to his own seriousness, a perfect fit.

But if Bud has no sense of limits it's precisely because he himself has been brutalised, first by a father who beat his mother to death, then by a police department that encourages and rewards his worst instincts.

Initially what makes Bud tick is in keeping with the simplistic psychologism tucked into a studio potboiler: his mother's death has turned him into a protector of women and the sometime killer of their male abusers. As is always the case with Ellroy's male characters, there is also something more complex at work here. Vengeance is Bud's quest but it's also his folly and, in Dudley Smith's hands, a means of control. ('I am most impressed with your punishment of woman beaters,' says Smith, before turning the younger detective into the thug he longs not to be.) Although Bud's reaction to the abuser at 4216 Evergreen – the deposed Santa, the volley of punches – can be seen as heroic, it's also an occasion for derision (from Stens), a peek into the primitive recesses of Bud's mind. It's not long after he beats the wife-beater that Bud meets Lynn, who's shopping for liquor as Dean Martin sings 'The Christmas Blues'. Outside in a car Lynn's pimp, Pierce Patchett, sits waiting with an anonymous redhead. Bud first notices Lynn (and she him – 'Merry Christmas to you, officer'), before catching sight of the redhead, who has an enormous bandage covering her nose. While Bud sees the women, he understands neither: for him, women are essentially, even naturally, victims in need of rescue and revenge. 'Somebody hit you?' he asks the redhead. Lynn assures him it's not what he thinks and the redhead wearily adds, 'You got the wrong idea, mister. I'm fine.' Bud does have it wrong; being a primitive, there's no way he can get it right.

If Bud looks every inch the 1950s Everyman, with his buzz-cut and ill-fitting brown jackets, Jack walks and talks like the star of his own show, from his alpine shoulders to his spectator shoes. He dresses like the main attraction, but Jack is a contract player, a hireling for three masters: the Los Angeles Police Department (LAPD); *Badge of Honor*, the television programme for which he serves as 'technical adviser'; and Hudgens, who features his arrests in *Hush-Hush* for payoffs and publicity. Jack is first seen nuzzling the neck of a plush brunette at a Christmas Eve party on the *Badge of Honor* set. As Lee Wiley sings 'I'm not the girl who cared about money', Jack nuzzles closer. 'What do you do on *Badge of Honor*,' asks the brunette. 'I teach [star] Brett Chase how to walk and talk like a cop.' Jack then sweetens his talk with a promise to give the woman the 'lowdown' on Robert Mitchum (who had been famously busted in 1948 on possession of

Badge of Honor, at home and in production

marijuana), only to be interrupted by Hudgens. The woman flounces off (*Hush-Hush* once flagged her as one of Hollywood's 'ingénue dykes') and the reporter and cop haggle over a payoff for an impending arrest. 'Jackie, it's Christmas,' whines Hudgens. 'No, it's not,' says Jack, 'it's felony possession of marijuana.' 'Actually,' Hudgens counters, 'it's circulation 36 thousand and climbing … once you whet the public's appetite for the truth, the sky's the limit.'

The arrest is pure Hollywood: as a voice announces 'the movie premiere of *When Worlds Collide*',[4] Jack and Hudgens assume position with a *Hush-Hush* photographer and a couple of cops waiting in the wings. Jack rehearses his blocking: 'All right, put your camera right *there*. When I walk out, I'll stop right *here*, you get the movie premiere in the background.' The newspaperman enthuses, 'I like it, I like it – The Movie Premiere Pot Bust.' 'Sid,' adds Jack, 'when I walk out the door I do not want those goddamn floodlights of yours in my eyes.' (He may be a hack director but he's a seasoned diva.) Inside the cottage, two young contract players with MGM giggle half-naked on a couch. Outside the front window, Hudgens stage whispers, 'Go, pop 'em,' and light bathes the interior, flooding the scene's hapless stars. Jack enters and delivers his line without conviction ('freeze, police') – he's played this part once too often. On the soundtrack, Dean Martin persists in singing the blues ('somebody wants you, somebody needs you') as Jack poses the actors in front of their last movie premiere before passing them to the cops who

'The Movie Premiere Pot Bust'

will take them to the now almost tragically named Hollywood police station. Back inside the cottage, Jack pockets the dope as Hudgens enters, polishing his lead for the next edition: 'It's Christmas Eve in the City of Angels …'

The novel is filled with such dispatches from the reporter, whose patois makes him the book's resident Walter Winchell, the influential gossip columnist.[5] Hudgens is a parasite but because gossip is the handmaiden of publicity (or maybe the other way around) he is a valuable parasite, since he's continually whetting the audience's movie appetite with slander. A minor cogwheel in Ellroy's outlandish machinations, he functions in the film more as a gutter Greek chorus of one. As with all the characters, he also registers as more human because DeVito cuts the sleaze with ingratiating geniality (somehow the actor's diminutive height makes him seem less malignant), and because of how he figures in Jack's transformation. In the novel and film, Jack takes up about as much narrative space as Bud and Ed but he's also very much a man apart, disconnected by his celebrity. (In the novel, he is also consumed by booze and Benzedrine.) As played by Kevin Spacey, the character is the most sympathetic of the men (he's funny, for one thing), with a moral reckoning that has the weight of an epiphany. Unlike Bud and Ed, who become whole only when they join forces, Jack arrives intact, even if his personality seems learned from Dean Martin, whose lush-life saunter and slur Spacey lightly borrows. Later, when Jack tries to protect a *Hush-Hush* target rather than sell him out, it isn't simply because he's rediscovered his conscience; it's because he's stopped playing a cop and become one.

Like Bud, Ed is first seen looking offscreen, but his focus is fixed on Captain Smith. It's Christmas Eve at the Hollywood station and a reporter is pumping Ed for a story on cops working holidays. As Ed feeds the public relations machine and Smith leads his men in 'Silver Bells', the reporter asks after two policemen recently injured in an assault. In uniform and glasses, Ed smilingly insists the men are fine, his answer as slick as his hair. He's an expert at hollow sincerity; he laughs too readily at Smith's jokes and flops after him down some stairs like a puppy. When the two are alone, the captain informs him that he's placed first out of twenty-three in the lieutenant's test. 'What will it be then?' asks Smith. Ed replies that he was thinking about the detective bureau. 'Edmund, you're a political animal. You have the eye for human weakness, but not the stomach.' Then, in a darkly funny, prescient exchange, the captain enquires just what sort of detective the younger man imagines himself. 'Would you be willing to beat a confession out of a suspect you knew to be guilty?' 'No,' Ed answers. 'Would you be willing to shoot a hardened criminal in the back in order to offset the chance that some lawyer—' Again, 'no.' 'Then,' says the captain, exasperated, 'for the love of God, don't be a detective.' The scene ends with a cheap parting shot: 'At least get rid of the glasses. I can't think of a single man in the bureau who wears them.'

There is a curious blandness to Ed in this scene, especially when contrasted with Bud and Jack's introductions. Smith's drill is as amusing as it is sinister, but Ed seems blank by comparison, devoid of reaction. The only thing notable about him is his insipid righteousness and almost feminine good looks. Dressed in crisp uniform blues, with his clerk glasses and sycophantic smile, Ed is the cop as politician, which in the logic of Ellroy's story makes him the most untrustworthy in the detective triumvirate. Pearce might have seemed too attractive for the role if it weren't for the way the actor uses his beauty against the character. At that point, the Australian actor was relatively unknown to American audiences,

Pearce and Cromwell

best known for playing a bitchy and very lovely drag queen in the camp film *The Adventures of Priscilla Queen of the Desert*.[6] The physical transformation from that film to *L.A. Confidential* is modest but nonetheless dramatic, a hallmark of this chameleon-like actor whose physiognomy seems to change with each role. As Ed, Pearce turns his face into a mask of right angles, one in which cheekbones seem sharp as knives, and similarly hardens his performance, refusing to solicit the audience's sympathies.

Ed's glasses code him as feminine and as a bureaucrat, an unhappy combination in a world of rule-breaking thugs like Bud. The character isn't far off from the one Ellroy created but the differences between the two versions are crucial. In the novel, each of the three detectives has a principal female love interest. Jack has a wife who tries and fails to save him; in the film, he has no great love other than himself, but his relationships with Hudgens and with a young male actor, both of whom are murdered, helps fill this absence. In the novel, Bud falls in love with Lynn and occasionally beds a woman named Inez Soto (who is reduced to a minor character for the film); in reverse, Ed falls in love with Inez and occasionally beds Lynn. Ed loses the most in the translation to the screen, including Inez and a tortured relationship with his father, a former detective turned entrepreneur. Instead, his long-dead father is now a hero cop murdered in the line of duty. Bereft of father and lover, Ed would barely register if it weren't for his antagonistic contempt and repressed

Marisol Padilla Sanchez as Inez Soto

desire for Bud. The homoeroticism gives the film an unexpected shiver but principally serves a narrative function in that it takes the place of Ed's excised affair with Inez and helps to justify his behaviour toward Bud and, later, toward Lynn.

The insinuation that Ed somehow doesn't look man enough for the job is tested shortly after Bud returns from the liquor store and Jack swans in with the recently arrested actors. Ed is serving as watch commander, manning the front desk. Jack tries to slip him a *Hush-Hush* payoff and as Ed refuses, a group of police bursts in with six Mexican detainees. While the prisoners are hustled to the holding tanks, word spreads that they have assaulted two patrolmen. Jack slides into his Dean Martin-inflected jocularity, teasingly announcing that one cop lost 'six pints of blood' while the other's in a coma. The drunken cops don't get that he's having fun at their expense and descend on the Mexicans. Bud and Jack follow suit while Ed is unceremoniously locked in a store room where he flails about, busily taking mental notes. The reporter grabs the story and the photographer a shot, thereupon turning a police riot into a front-page news headline, 'Bloody Christmas'.

In 1997, six years after the assault on Rodney King, the image of Los Angeles police beating prisoners was a familiar one to audiences around the world. King was the black Angeleno who in 1991 was stopped by California highway patrol officers for speeding, an infraction that ultimately attracted twenty-seven officers, including twenty-three

'Bloody Christmas'

from the LAPD, along with a helicopter equipped with the floodlights
that would illuminate the scene for amateur-video posterity. The
eventual acquittal of the officers charged in the beating resulted in one
of the worst civil disturbances in United States history. Although it was
arguably the biggest stain on the LAPD's record, it was by no means the
only one. The decade before the real 'Bloody Christmas', the Zoot Suit
Riots found city police standing idly by as thousands of white servicemen
roamed the city beating young blacks and Mexican Americans. The
department had been historically plagued by the sort of corruption that
helped create the communities it served, and after the Second World
War it hit a particularly rough patch. In 1949, a Grand Jury empanelled
to investigate police corruption concluded, 'The alarming increase in the
number of unsolved murders and other major crimes reflects
ineffectiveness in law enforcement agencies and the Courts, that should
not be tolerated ...'

William Parker became the new chief the following year, a position
he held until his death in 1966. (A minor character in the novel, he is
identified in the film simply as the 'police chief'.) It was Parker who
instituted the infamous military model for the LAPD that would become
known as 'the most aggressive police department in the country', as his

Bob Hope and Jane
Russell celebrate the
LAPD with Chief Parker,
1952

protégé and later successor Daryl Gates once put it.[7] Yet even as the organisation learned one lesson from the military, it learned another, equally significant, lesson from Hollywood: public relations. According to its gadfly historian Joe Domanick, the LAPD was exceptionally innovative when it came to self-promotion. From the 1930s on, it produced fund-raising stage shows hosted by the likes of Bob Hope; during the 1940s, its public relations unit expanded into movies and produced titles such as *Motors on Parade*, extolling the motorcycle squad. By 1955, the unit had a new name – the Public Information division – and some twenty officers who planted positive stories, vetted television police shows such as *Dragnet* and wrote most of Parker's speeches.[8]

In *L.A. Confidential*, 'Bloody Christmas' isn't a stain on the police – it's a public-relations crisis. This becomes explicit in a sequence following the riot that serves as a coda to the detective introductions and places the three men firmly within the story's grid of power. The section begins with the chief reading a headline from a newspaper, declaring: '"Bloody Christmas". The press love to label.' Flanked by District Attorney Ellis Loew and Dudley Smith, respective embodiments of Los Angeles Law and Order, the chief subsequently negotiates the future of the film's three detectives, as well as that of the city itself. One by one, Bud, Ed and Jack are asked to testify against other officers involved in the riot. Bud declines; he's suspended but reinstated soon afterward when Smith assigns him to strong-arm detail in his rogue outfit, the 'Mobster Squad'. As if to prove himself the 'political animal' Smith identified, Ed engineers a cover-up that leads to his promotion to detective lieutenant and earns Jack just a brief suspension. In exchange for his testimony, Jack is reassigned from his post in the Narcotics division to Vice and temporarily relieved of his gig on *Badge of Honor*. When Smith asks Ed if he's prepared to be despised by every man on the force, he answers, 'Yes, sir. I am.' With this exchange, the old LAPD comes face to face with the new, a department every bit as savage as the old but now shrewdly political. The blueprints for the new LAPD and for what Loew calls 'the City of the Future' have been drawn.

On the beat: Bud; an LAPD billboard; and Ed

The novel *L.A. Confidential* ends in 1958, the same year that the body of James Ellroy's mother, Geneva ('Jean') Hilliker Ellroy, was found in an ivy thicket in the small town of El Monte, some twelve miles east of downtown Los Angeles. Her son was ten. Born in L.A., James Ellroy had lived weekdays with his mother, a 43-year-old divorced redhead who worked as a registered nurse in an aircraft-parts plant, one of the region's booming industries. He spent weekends in Los Angeles with his father, Armand, a one-time business manager who lived on the ragged fringe of a wealthy neighbourhood called Hancock Park. On Sunday, 22 June 1958, some kids on their way to baseball practice stumbled across Jean's body. She had been raped, then strangled; one of her stockings was wrapped around her neck, while the other was puddled about an ankle. That afternoon, James returned home alone from a weekend spent with his father, and was greeted by flanks of police and journalists. Years later, in *My Dark Places*, his devastating account of his mother's life and death, and his subsequent attempt to solve the murder, he wrote: 'A man took me aside and kneeled down to my level. He said, "Son, your mother's been killed."'[9] Shortly thereafter, a photographer for the *Los Angeles Times* posed the boy at a workbench holding an awl and took his picture. The shot ran the next morning.

Over the years, various reporters and documentary film-makers have reconstructed Ellroy's history, as has the author himself, most unsparingly in *My Dark Places*. In that book, Ellroy recounts his early struggle to live with his mother's violent death, first as a voracious consumer of pop crime, then as a juvenile delinquent. (A self-described panty sniffer, he broke into houses for kicks and lingerie.) Following Jean's murder, Ellroy went to live with his father, where he passed much of the time watching crime shows on television and immersing himself in crime fiction. Initially his taste ran to squeaky-clean avengers such as the Hardy Boys before, on his father's recommendation, he graduated to Mickey Spillane. On his eleventh birthday, less than a year after his mother's death, for reasons the adult Ellroy can't explain, Armand gave his son a copy of *The Badge*, a panegyric to the LAPD written by Jack Webb, the auteur and monotone star of the hit television drama, *Dragnet*.[10] At once a police procedural, a

lurid exposé and an apologia for the department, the book was written in the actor's trademark staccato ('just the facts') and leans heavily on morbid true-crime stories about doomed lonely women. As Ellroy wrote in *My Dark Places*, 'I read Jack Webb's account of the Black Dahlia murder case. It sent me way off the deep end.'[11]

Before she was a celebrity corpse, the Black Dahlia had been Elizabeth Short. Strikingly beautiful, with pale eyes and deep black hair, Short moved to Los Angeles to work in the movies. She won a beauty contest ('The Camp Cutie of Camp Cook'), kept company with actors on the hustle and, as with most Hollywood hopefuls, never got much of anywhere. Her jet-coloured hair and her then-eccentric fondness for wearing black clothes inspired her sobriquet; admiring servicemen had bequeathed it on Short following the release of the Veronica Lake–Alan Ladd film, *The Blue Dahlia*. Short had wanted to be in movies not because of any evident interest in acting, but because different people along the way had told her she had the looks to make it, the irony being that it was her looks that probably helped get her killed. Wildly, baroquely grotesque, the murder gripped Los Angeles. A housewife pushing a stroller found the body in the derelict lot on 15 January 1947. As the autopsy report revealed, Short had been tortured, human excrement had been forced down her throat and, while still alive, she had been cut in half at the waist. It's no wonder that the housewife first thought she had stumbled across a store mannequin – the flesh had a waxy sheen and all the woman saw was the

severed lower half. The killer hadn't simply murdered Short, he (or she) had turned her body into an object.

The murder was horrible but it was spectacularly, cinematically horrible – the stuff of Cornell Woolrich novels and the tough, shadow-strafed American movies that the French had recently christened *noir*. Following the identification of the body, a local reporter named Sid Hughes (the name echoes that of Sid Hudgens) located a mug shot of Short that had been taken four years earlier, after she'd been arrested for under-age drinking. 'That gal's picture', said Hughes, 'could've been used on a magazine cover. She had a haunting kind of beauty – those eyes staring far off, it's the truth – those lips talked sex and mystery without even moving.'[12] Short was a fantastic pin-up, even if she was dead – the low-rent equivalent of the film noir goddess Laura, the woman men fall for even in death. Although the local press couldn't get enough of it, the murder was too gruesome for the Hollywood studios, at least while the Production Code was in effect. Even without big-screen immortality it seeped into the Los Angeles groundwater for decades, feeding and sustaining the city's reputation as a purgatory in which the desire for fame can be lethal. A lot of things define a city, including its crimes; few have defined a city as damnably as the murder of Elizabeth Short.

It is easy to see what it was about the case that gripped James Ellroy's imagination and kept hold of it for years. As with Short, Jean Ellroy had been beautiful, a pageant queen (America's 'Most Charming Redhead'), a

Elizabeth Short alive; the Black Dahlia dead

magnet for men. And, as with Short, she had been sexually violated, then murdered, her body abandoned. The violence visited upon Short was more outrageous, Grand Guignol in its extremity, but it didn't matter; the crimes were similar enough to do their black magic on the boy. In time, the women's bodies effectively merged into one – one dead, brutally and sexually violated woman – becoming, effectively, a projection on which the future writer could, and later did, inscribe his own violent stories. In *My Dark Places*, Ellroy wrote of the women who subsequently came into his life, 'I never downscaled my romantic expectations.' He'd loved and hated his mother with equal passion, spied on her in the bathroom, dreamed and fantasised about her, and then she was dead. 'I went at women less ferociously over time,' he confessed. 'I learned to disguise my hunger. That hunger went straight into my books. They got more and more obsessive. I was burning a lifelong torch with three flames. My mother. The Dahlia. The woman I knew God would give me.'[13]

The murders of Jean Ellroy and Elizabeth Short inform much of Ellroy's work, most directly in his fictionalised account of the Dahlia case. A clammy fever dream dedicated to his mother ('Twenty-nine Years Later, This Valediction in Blood') and published in 1987, *The Black Dahlia* is the first volume the L.A. Quartet, a sweeping, phantasmagoric series about the post-war city that begins in 1947 and ends in 1959. (If time were marked by movie releases, the quartet would begin with *Out of the Past* and end with *Touch of Evil*.) Taken together, the books, rich in history and churning with the muck of the human condition, present a view of Los Angeles that's steeped in nihilism and distinctly at odds with the usual booster jive of the sort peddled by Sid Hudgens. The Dahlia murder and its aftershocks on the city reverberate through *L.A. Confidential*, which is similarly littered with corpses and all manner of tortured flesh. For reasons of narrative economy the dead accumulate at a slower rate in the film than the novel. And still the bodies fall, with most of Ellroy's violence condensed into a single mass murder at the Nite Owl coffee shop, where among the victims lies Susan Lefferts, the redhead Bud White noticed on Christmas Eve.

In the film, Lefferts, a prostitute working for Pierce Patchett, has recently undergone plastic surgery to further her resemblance to the movie star, Rita Hayworth, who – like Ellroy's mother – was also a redhead. After Lefferts is delivered to the morgue, the LAPD brings her mother in to identify the body, but the older woman doesn't recognise Susan because of the surgery and because she knew her daughter as a blonde. It isn't until an attendant lifts the sheet draping the corpse and Mrs Lefferts sees a birthmark adorning its hip that she can make the identification. (Elizabeth Short's mother and sister identified her body by a birthmark, as well.) The pathos of a woman who cannot recognise her own dead child is startling, as are the bodies – mostly young, mostly female – who, on arriving in Los Angeles, transform beyond recognition. Significantly, in the novel Susan Lefferts is neither a prostitute nor a redhead; she's a girlfriend who happens to land in the proverbial wrong place at the proverbial wrong time. By turning the character into one of Patchett's movie-star lookalikes, the film underscores the link between Hollywood and prostitution, and summons up the memory of the dead women in Ellroy's personal mausoleum: Jean Ellroy, Elizabeth Short, Rita Hayworth.

For about three or four years, beginning in the late 1940s, Armand Ellroy worked as the business manager for Hayworth, whose popularity as the erotic queen of Hollywood took on newfound notoriety when she began a whirlwind romance with the Aly Khan. (Armand's son says his

'You've got the wrong idea, mister.'

father helped arrange the wedding.) The star eventually fired her business manager for unspecified reasons, although that didn't stop the senior Ellroy from trading on their relationship. For years afterward he would brag to his son that he hadn't just worked for Hayworth, he had slept with her or, in a vivid locution shared by father and son, 'poured [her] the pork'. She would never know it, of course, but the actress figured as a crucial high point in the older Ellroy's employment history and personal mythology, perfuming him – and by extension the entire family – with a certain irresistible glamour. No matter what the real truth of Armand's more licentious claims – and no matter that, in the end, it was glamour by proxy – Rita Hayworth had imprinted the Ellroy family with some sort of celebrity, which wafted through their lives like an unarticulated promise. It's a promise that hangs over Los Angeles like smog.

In *Down and Out in Paris and London*, George Orwell wrote that the waiters working in elite restaurants don't just serve their 'betters', they leech them:

His work gives him the mentality, not of a workman, but of a snob. He lives perpetually in sight of rich people, stands at their tables, listens to their conversations, sucks up to them with smiles and discreet little jokes. He has the pleasure of spending money by proxy. Moreover, there is always the chance that he may become rich himself.[14]

In Los Angeles, celebrity isn't the exclusive province of the rich and the famous (or infamous); it belongs to everyone – to the celebrity agents, managers and publicists but also to the celebrity realtors, gardeners and dog-walkers. By working for Hayworth, Armand Ellroy earned a guest pass to fame that allowed him to rub shoulders with the elite (like Hayworth) and befriend others on the fade (like Mickey Rooney). For Jean Ellroy, who once worked as a nurse for ZaSu Pitts when the silent-screen actress had fallen on hard boozing times, celebrity by proxy was less appealing. It was considerably less so for her son, who, as an adult, caddied at one of L.A.'s most exclusive golf courses, hauling clubs for stars such as Robert Stack. Years later, Stack, then host for the true-crime

television programme *Unsolved Mysteries*, presented the Jean Ellroy case to a new audience; James Ellroy says when he saw who the show's host was he just laughed.

Jean Ellroy's death rated only a brief period of time as Los Angeles news. Her son discovered as much when he retraced the investigation into his mother's murder. 'The L.A. papers ran the sketch of the suspect and dropped the story cold,' he wrote in *My Dark Places*. 'The redhead never clicked as a victim. The Lana Turner/Cheryl Crane/Johnny Stompanato case hogged all the headlines.'[15] A muscle man for Mickey Cohen and the boyfriend of movie star Lana Turner, Stompanato is a minor figure in the novel of *L.A. Confidential* but carries more weight in the film, embodying not merely the corruption of the mob but that of Hollywood. To emphasise the point, in a scene not in the novel, Ed even mistakes the 'real' Lana Turner, nestled in a restaurant booth with Stompanato, for a prostitute, believing her to belong to Pierce Patchett's stable. As it happens, the actual Turner–Stompanato affair was as sordid as any Poverty Row cheapie: on 4 April 1958, Turner's fourteen-year-old daughter, Cheryl Crane, stabbed Stompanato to death as her mother looked on. Crane got off; so did her mother, who the next year went on to star in the aptly titled *Imitation of Life*.

Perversely, soon after Ellroy launched the re-investigation of his mother's death, the headlines were dominated by yet more celebrity: the murders of Ronald Goldman and O. J. Simpson's wife, Nicole. Ellroy had decided to look into his mother's case after his wife, writer Helen Knode,

Imitation of life: the 'real' Lana Turner with Stompanato, Ed, and Jack

The actual Turner with
Stompanato and
daughter Cheryl Crane,
1958

stumbled over the posed newspaper photograph of the young Ellroy taken
on the day he learned of his mother's death. The picture became a catalyst
for Ellroy, a way into his and his mother's past; in some respects, the
investigation seemed like a bid at an exorcism. James Ellroy had lived with
the mythical Jean Ellroy four times longer than he had ever lived with the
flesh-and-blood woman; he wanted to retrieve the real woman from the
lies and myths that had, since her death, wrapped about her like a shroud.
Before she was murdered Ellroy's father had repeatedly told his son that
his dead ex-wife was 'a drunk and a whore'. The malevolence of the attack
is breathtaking and lingered long after her death. In the end, as pitiless as
he could sometimes be toward his father, who died when the son was
seventeen, Ellroy lets Armand off easy in *My Dark Places*. Given that after
the murder they only had each other, who could blame him? Still, there
remains something intently bleak in the way the father helped nourish his
son's obsession with his mother, which having started off along fairly
routine oedipal lines would, with her murder, grow progressively kinkier.

You get a sense of just how kinky in some of his fiction. In *The Black
Dahlia*, Ellroy fashions a complex narrative in which the titular dead
woman is at once a whore and a cipher, a blur of a woman that one
character after another tries to fill with fantasy. In his exhaustively

researched book on the murder, John Gilmore paints a different, less sensationalistic picture of the real Elizabeth Short as a lost young woman who, while almost frenetic in her relationships with men, tried to avoid intimate contact because of her underdeveloped genitalia. Jean Ellroy, by contrast, was an ordinary woman and it is her very ordinariness that makes her so tragic – that, and her son's love. She was, without complication, a beautiful, divorced woman and mother. She drank too much, too often, and sometimes she enjoyed the company of men; then, she was murdered. When you ask Ellroy, now fifty-five, to tell you about the child he was at the time of his mother's death, the kid things he did and watched and read, the past rushes into the room with stunning intensity. He doesn't possess total memory, but he can summon up old details and long-gone decades with such lapidary precision that you realise one of the reasons he likes to write about the past is that he never fully left it. The man was born in 1948 but the writer was born the day his mother died.

'I recall that prelude to my mother's death in June of '58 with great clarity,' said Ellroy:

I went to a whole string of movies that I recall very vividly during this time frame, one of them was the cheap-o film noir *Plunder Road*. Multiple, first-person stream-of-consciousness as all these losers hurtle toward their fate. They rob a train with bullion headed for Fort Knox. One of the losers rendezvous with his girlfriend and another loser, and they weld the gold onto a bumper of a car. They're going to drive down to T.J. [Tijuana] and they get in a fender bender on the Hollywood Freeway. An alert policeman sees the gold, the girlfriend starts screaming and the two men run to their deaths off a freeway embankment with the cops shooting them. In other words, there's the great single noir theme: you're fucked. And young Ellroy, he's very, very impressed. You know, he's a kid from a broken home, he's nine years old and he's ahead of the arc in human experience at this stage of the game.

So, the old man would come out to El Monte, he'd pick me up on Saturday morning or Friday night, bring me back on Sunday morning or Sunday afternoon, sans church. We saw a string of Budd Boetticher

Westerns – *Buchanan Rides Alone* and *Seven Men From N   ow* – at the Iris Theater on Hollywood Boulevard. And *Alfred Hitchcock Presents* was on every Sunday night. Hitchcock at the end of ever show would advertise his most recent film, and it was *Vertigo*. So here is this masterpiece of sexual obsession, and I saw *that* about two weekends before my mother was killed. In the meantime, what's interesting about all this is that I'm dead-flat obsessed with her, in the manner I described in *My Dark Places*: you know, I'm sniffing her undies. She wears Tweed perfume and I poured some on a handkerchief so I could smell her, brought it to school with me, was sniffing it. We had this little crummy bathroom and my mother didn't flaunt her nudity but she didn't hide it, either. I would take the world's longest baths in hopes that she'd come in and take a leak. I'm completely obsessed with her. I end that section in *My Dark Places* with 'I hated her and lusted for her and then she was dead.' You know, *bam*. From that point on, it was just crime and me.[16]

2 Red Harvest

We know the detective; we've seen him before. If he's in business for himself, he wears off-the-rack suits, a belted trench coat and maybe a gun. Once upon a time, he wore a fedora. Sometimes he still smokes, he almost always still drinks – booze, straight up or on the rocks, taken in gulps or in long ruminative sips. If he works for the police, he generally dresses worse but drinks, smokes and dies more or less the same. He is, finally, a predator – of men, of women, of knowledge – and the more he wants, the more he's wanted in return, although with him desire isn't often expressed with shudders of pleasure but of pain. That, of course, is part of his allure – the slaps, the blows, the spasmodic fury, the open wounds, the streams of spittle, the spouts of blood. 'I began to throw my right fist into him,' says Dashiell Hammett's Continental Op in the 1924 short story, 'Women, Politics and Murder'. 'I liked that. His belly was flabby, and it got softer every time I hit it. I hit it often.'[17]

A staple in American fiction since the mid-nineteenth century, the detective has been a staple of American cinema since the early 1930s. In 1941, John Huston brought Hammett's Sam Spade to the screen with *The Maltese Falcon*, thereupon introducing the hard-boiled variant that would persevere into the 1950s, languish to the point of irrelevancy during the 1960s, only to be resurrected by *Dirty Harry* in 1972.[18] In the three decades since, the detective has continued to bring order to chaos even as he has also left behind the confines of the thriller, shedding much of his metaphysical burden in the process. A version of this type – deracinated, at times pushed past parody into burlesque – has so dominated American movies that familiar genre categories such as the Western or science fiction have become subordinate to the rubric of 'the action movie'. Their edge blunted in exchange for grim comedy and blockbuster returns, the heroes in these films nonetheless retain what can seem like a specifically American imperative for solving conflict and for tying up loose narrative ends with violence. In literature, all the while, the type strains to defy exhaustion by assuming a miscellany of post-modern identities – the female gumshoe, the Native American investigator and the like, all of which restlessly circle about the white male paradigm no matter how far afield they stray.

In his oft-quoted 1944 essay 'The Simple Art of Murder', Raymond Chandler wrote that the detective 'must be, to use a rather weathered phrase, a man of honor, by instinct, by inevitability, without thought of it, and certainly without saying it'.[19] Chandler's ostensible subject was the detective story but the actual matter at hand was the worth of the genre, and the essay bristles with the fury of a great writer working in a form the literary establishment refused to take seriously. As Edmund Wilson carped in one his volleys across the cultural battlefield, 'Who Cares Who Killed Roger Ackroyd?' The critic deemed Chandler better than most of his ilk principally because his work didn't belong to the school of the 'old-fashioned detective novel'.[20] Wilson didn't think much of this school but, then, neither did Chandler, who favoured Dashiell Hammett's example. Hammett, wrote Chandler, 'took murder out of the Venetian vase and dropped it into the alley … gave murder back to the kind of people that commit it for reasons, not just to provide a corpse; and with the means at hand, not with hand-wrought duelling pistols, curare, and tropical fish'.[21] Equally, or perhaps more meaningfully to Chandler, Hammett proved that 'the detective story can be important writing', which was, of course, as self-serving a statement as it was true.

The defensive tone of Chandler's most famous essay, along with its gusts of grandiloquence, indicates that he didn't much revel in his status as literary outcast. In his work, murder is committed in the same alley where Hammett dropped it, but with a more self-conscious striving toward high literature. At the opening of *The Big Sleep*, Philip Marlowe walks up to a rich man's house where he notices a stained-glass panel of a knight trying to rescue a damsel. Marlowe considers that if he lived in the huose he would one day have to climb up to help, since the knight 'didn't seem to be really trying', but the impulse is purely ironic, a gesture of self-conscious cool on the part of the author and his character.[22] In contrast, in the Continental Op story 'The Main Death', when Hammett's operative walks into a rich man's house and a beautiful young woman puts down a copy of *The Sun Also Rises*, neither the Op nor Hammett bothers to pick it up again. The Hemingway reference is tossed into the story like an olive into a gin martini, where it sits, essential but also forgotten.

Ellroy betrays none of Chandler's defensiveness or high-culture squeamishness toward Hammett's alley, but then history and criticism are on his side. One of the more profound differences between Chandler and Ellroy springs from the changed critical reception of genre literature. For Chandler, whose first novel was published in 1939, the detective's morality seems inseparable from – even predicated on – the baseness of his milieu. The detective's morality not only justifies the squalid nature of his calling; it saves the author, too, from the accusation of exploitation and the imprimatur of pure pulp. In the L.A. Quartet, the detectives are often as brutal as the criminals they chase; there is nothing in Ellroy's chthonic worldview (much less that of his detectives) which jibes with the prescriptions of 'The Simple Art of Murder'. If anything, the three detectives of *L.A. Confidential* play out like rebuttals to Chandler's moral loner. There is nothing honourable about them; they are heroes of a sort because of – not despite – their imperfect humanity. At once nostalgic and anti-nostalgic, redeemable and unforgiven, they are the writer's imaginary men – envisioned through a scrim of pop culture and terrible longing, embodiments of the moment at which the author came of cruel age.

In contrast to classic whodunits, in which crime happens, then resolution, the action in *L.A. Confidential* unfolds simultaneously with the narrative. The novel opens with a brief prologue that introduces Dudley Smith along with an ex-cop named Buzz Meeks, a central character in the quartet's proceeding novel, *The Big Nowhere*. Without ceremony, the prologue presents Smith in the role of villain the moment he fatally shoots Meeks, a role that the film keeps hidden until about two-thirds of the way in, when he does the same thing to Jack Vincennes. Meeks is killed (in book and film both) for stealing heroin from Smith, who's conspiring to take over the dirty business of the imprisoned Mickey Cohen. In the film, Meeks first appears as Pierce Patchett's bodyguard (later he becomes a rat-bitten corpse), and helps to connect the pimp with Smith, a utility he doesn't serve in the novel. Ellroy's byzantine plot comprises two seemingly disparate strands that knit together in the final pages. The first strand features Smith, Patchett and organised crime, while the second encompasses a macabre conspiracy involving, among others, Patchett; Raymond Dieterling, a Disney-like entertainment magnate; and Ed's father, Preston Exley, a former policeman turned big-builder and aspiring politician.

During the 1930s (the decade, parenthetically, in which Disney became a household name), Dieterling sacrificed one of his sons to conceal the sins of a favoured second, a serial child-killer. He had handed over the innocent child for execution to an unwitting Preston Exley, while secreting the guilty boy into hiding. (After going underground in L.A., the silver-spoon maniac endures multiple plastic surgeries, creates snuff-style porn and works as a technician on the set of *Badge of Honor*, which says as much about Ellroy's imagination as his feelings about his home town.) Thus joined, Dieterling and Preston go on to control Los Angeles paralleled by Patchett and Smith – a collusion of blood in which the city's entire infrastructure is implicated. For Ellroy, the city's original sin is built on filicide, a murderous bond echoed by other father–son relationships, from white men who call grown black men 'son' to the detectives, like Bud and Jack, who repeatedly call Smith 'Dud', one vowel away from 'Dad'. Although the three detectives untangle the conspiracies, in the process Jack dies, Bud almost dies and Ed renounces his father ('Goddamn you for the bad things you made me'). Ed tries to arrest Preston, but the elder Exley commits suicide alongside Dieterling and Inez Soto.

L.A. Confidential is a novel about a lot of things – Los Angeles, Hollywood, racism, sexism, capitalism and any number of other assorted evils – but at its core are sons confronting the sins of their fathers. In their screenplay, Hanson and Helgeland eliminate the Preston, Dieterling, Soto triangle, thereby considerably attenuating the story's father-and-son theme. In the film, Ed has been transformed into an avenger of the wrong done to Preston Exley, now a cop shot down by a purse snatcher, rather than an avenger of the wrongs committed by his father. The film's Ed keeps the memory of his father burning by calling the unknown assailant

'Rollo Tomasi', a fabricated name that has become the son's cause and excuse.[23] 'Rollo Tomasi is the reason I became a cop,' Ed tells Jack. 'I wanted to catch the guys who thought they could get away with it.' For Ed, the pursuit of evil and of justice by any means helps fill the absence left by his dead father. As with Bud, whose life is an endless rampage on behalf of his murdered mother, Ed is eternally stuffing this absence with the bodies of other victims and perpetrators. Women spill tears in their melodramas, these men spill blood. Still, no matter how many of the innocent they avenge and how many of the guilty they punish, Bud and Ed are always left wanting more – theirs is a ravenous hunger.

The novel begins with dead bodies and it's dead bodies that stoke the narrative. A cop kills a former cop for drugs stolen from a gangster, turmoil that ripples over the city like blast waves. In the film, the devastation is set in motion by the Nite Owl massacre. 'Bodies,' writes Ellroy, 'a blood-soaked pile on the floor. Brains, blood and buckshot on the walls. Blood two feet deep collecting in a drainage trough. Dozens of shotgun shells floating in blood.'[24] It happens some thirty minutes after the start mark, shortly after the three detectives have assumed their new posts following Bloody Christmas. Reunited with his gun and badge, Bud has been kept busy in the Mobster Squad. Now one of Smith's personal goons, he helps rout gangsters who, in the wake of Mickey Cohen's imprisonment, have started to stake claims on the city. In an abandoned motor inn called the Victory Motel, Bud pounds away at would-be racketeers while Smith delivers the departmental *coup de grâce*: 'Los Angeles is organised-crime free. And the Chief wants to keep it that way.' Jack, meanwhile, has landed at Vice, where he's come across high-end pornography stamped with the same 'Fleur-de-Lis' emblem he saw on a business card found at the Movie Premiere Pot Bust. The only one of the detectives who seems remotely satisfied is Ed, now ensconced in his new berth in Homicide, having stepped into the position just as Stensland, Bud's partner, has been dismissed.

Alone in Homicide at two in the morning, Ed takes a call from the dispatcher. 'You've got a homicide,' a female voice crackles over the

squawk box. 'Downtown Division, the Nite Owl coffee shop.' What
follows is a tour de force of atmosphere and camerawork, and a narrative
sleight of hand in which the film's every suggestion of seductive nostalgia
is washed away in blood. Ed arrives outside the Nite Owl, where he's met
by a flustered young patrolman who had stopped for coffee and instead
discovered a corpse. Instructing the cop to secure the area ('no one comes
through the front door'), Ed approaches the entrance, at which point the
camera cuts inside the coffee shop so that it can capture him as he enters.
He does so, pulling the smudged glass door open with a handkerchief.
Hidden behind his glasses and Brilliantined hair, tweed jacket, sweater
vest and tie, the young lieutenant looks more like an adjunct professor
than a big-city detective, which means he looks seriously ill-prepared for
the situation in which he's landed. He begins his slow walk through the
crime scene and as he does, composer Jerry Goldsmith's soundtrack cues

Forbidden pleasures; Mobster Squad headquarters

in with some minor piano chords that pound out a tattoo of fearful anticipation.

After sizing Ed up (*who* is this?), the camera again assumes his point of view. Charred meat smokes on the griddle as the dead cook lies slumped below. Ed scans the coffee shop, narrowing in on a table with an overturned chair that looks as if it had been hurriedly vacated. There are dirty cups and a plate on the table, along with a ketchup bottle the same colour as a nearby blotch of blood on the wall. More blood has been scuffed across the linoleum, creating a trail that leads out of a back door. Unruffled, nearly devoid of expression, Ed follows the trail into a dingy hallway, then into a men's bathroom. He pushes open the door and as he does the camera arcs over his right shoulder to peer at five bodies stacked in a puddle of blood, more red splashed across the surrounding walls for an action painting of violence and death. The film cuts to Ed's face, closer now, the mask rigid

The Nite Owl: coffee shop turned charnel house

save for the twitch near his mouth; abruptly, there's a cut to Smith, who's arrived outside and is busily barking orders to a contingent of other officers. Joining Smith, Ed says, 'Sir, I took the call, it's my case.' Smith refuses to cede authority and makes Ed second in command. The two have their picture taken by a news photographer, but not before Ed removes his glasses and wipes the twitch off his jaw. The scene ends shortly after the police realise that one of the victims is Stensland.

There is a striking preternatural quiet to the Nite Owl discovery scene, a stillness that indicates shifts in mood and in aesthetics. Ed's footfalls are barely audible and the ambient noise is dominated by two aural 'close-ups', one at the start of the walk-through (meat sizzling and pots boiling on the abandoned stove) and one at the end (the squeak and squeal of the men's bathroom door being pushed open). The music initially underscores Ed's movements but, when a trumpet and some skittish strings chime in, seems more syncopated to the pulse of a thudding heart than to footfalls. Mounted principally on a dolly, the camera moves fluidly forward through the long space as Ed does his walk-through, the image restlessly moving between long shots and medium close-ups. The point of view is equally restive, slipping from third to first person as the image alternates between shots of Ed as he looks over the coffee shop and, more unusually, shots that directly show us what he's looking at, as if the camera were seeing with his eyes. The oscillation in points of view tightens the tension, since we are continually invited to assume Ed's place even if we don't want to. Taken together, the differing views are instrumental in Hanson's assumption of a bolder, more expressionistic visual style.

Because of Ellroy's dense plotting, Hanson and Helgeland spend the first half an hour of the film establishing the three detectives in their respective and shared milieus. Hanson maintains a light directorial touch throughout the preliminaries, using familiar devices such as montage and voiceover to get across, as expediently and as seamlessly as possible, a daunting amount of information. With the introductions over, however, he starts to make the film his own, which is what he does at the Nite Owl, the scene in which *L.A. Confidential* ceases to belong to James Ellroy and becomes Curtis Hanson's. Thereafter, the story will be secondary to the

people pushing it forward, secondary to how shadows fall across faces, to how music fills rooms, to the ways in which the characters circle one another and to how the camera moves through space. Paring away Ellroy's narrative liberates Hanson, freeing him to lavish attention on the characters, to burrow into their heads and into their scenes, so that what matters isn't only that Bud beats other men for a living but the self-contempt which ripples across his face when he does. Or that when Lynn first invites Bud into her bedroom – her own, not the one she keeps for the 'suckers' – the book on her end table is M. F. K. Fisher's *How to Cook a Wolf*.[25]

In its exacting period detail *L.A Confidential* looks and moves like a meticulous simulation despite the nod at Fisher, which probably wouldn't have made it into a Hollywood film of the early 1950s, and especially despite the expletives and the representation of the LAPD, which certainly wouldn't have. Hanson's film looks like a genuine artefact but with the social and political filters off. The epithets and the police brutality add to the overall verisimilitude and make the re-creation seem all the more authentic. At the same time, if those were the only adjustments, they would play more like sops to the sensibilities of the modern audience, which expects its historical stories delivered in a grittier key. Given what we know now, a story about Los Angeles without the expletives, the racism, the sex and the cynicism, even circa the early 1950s, would likely seem off to contemporary viewers, the stuff of parody. Simply fouling up the characters' behaviour and the language, as is often the case with period movies, is in itself unremarkable, since what finally matters is the underlying image, not simply the dirt smeared over it.

Films set in the past are dependent on the audience's nostalgic relationship to the re-created era, whether that relationship is critical or not, and whether the relationship is rooted in the past or manufactured in the present. Even films that purport to dismantle the past often succumb to nostalgia out of expectations that require history to be teleological and entertaining (and woe to those that fail on either count). Roman Polanski's *Chinatown* (1974), while betraying little sentimentalism about the Los Angeles of the 1930s, nonetheless betrays a yearning for a moment in which race and gender are as irrelevant (or invisible) as they were during the classic studio era. Less a deconstruction of the classic detective narrative than a surrender, the film is unable to sustain its social critique because its narrative never escapes the logic of genre. The doomed character played by Faye Dunaway remains a classic femme fatale until the moment of her death when she becomes one of cinema's consummate female victims. Like Chinatown itself, the neighbourhood in which she dies, the character is a metaphor for life's mystery, an abyss of Otherness not much different from the Chinese characters who hover at the film's periphery as servants, as gawking bystanders and as punch lines (the 'screwing just like a Chinaman' joke).

The film's famous capitulation to hopelessness – 'Forget it, Jake. It's Chinatown' – is the stoic's lament, an acknowledgment that the world is unknowable and irrational, and that nothing can be done about any of it. For Ellroy, the world is anything but unknowable. It is a dark and despairing place but essentially recognisable, a world of crime and punishment in which there are no true mysteries, only unsolved cases. To read *L.A. Confidential* is to understand Ellroy as a kind of prisoner of a time and place whose only escape is to construct a parallel world, a shadow Los Angeles in which he can run furiously amok. This is perhaps why there is so little evident everyday human pleasure in Ellroy's Los Angeles (in their Hobbesian war of all against all, the characters fight more than they eat), only the pleasure of the writer's own imagination, his endless words. A line in the film perfectly captures this quality of Ellroy's passionate destruction: when Bud asks Ed if he's really willing to relinquish everything he's built up in order to take down Smith, Exley answers 'with a wrecking ball'.

Hanson had said that he wanted *L.A. Confidential* to 'be true to the period but also feel contemporary'. He was clear about not wanting to make a neo-noir, one of those pastiches in which noir is empty posturing rather than a cry of despair. He wanted to capture the city of 'his childhood memories' and 'of manufactured illusion'.[26] To animate these phantoms, Hanson, working with director of photography Dante Spinotti and production designer Jeannine Oppewall, devised a visual style that was as lustrous as a studio classic but without sentimentalism. Before going into production, Hanson and Oppewall had, unbeknown to the other, each taken in a retrospective of the work of photographer Robert Frank, a gift of serendipity that worked its way into the film. Frank's

Alone in 1950s America, the empty Nite Owl and Ed

application of extant light in his 1958 book *The Americans* finds a corollary in *L.A. Confidential*, where much of the key light was supplied by practical sources such as table lamps and overhead fluorescent fixtures.[27]

The film seems to have been influenced by something less tangible in Frank's work, as well. Frank took the photographs while travelling across the country during 1955 and 1956, and taken together his images of people in diners, factories and staring outward next to tattered American flags create a vision of an isolated, melancholic people lost in a mood distinctly at odds with the Eisenhower moment. In describing the impact of *The Americans*, critic John Szarkowski once wrote,

The more distressing new quality of Frank's pictures was their equivocating indirection, their reluctance to state clearly and simply either their subject or their moral. Like a prophet reciting enigmas, Frank seemed to photograph around the periphery of the true subject, showing us things tangential to it, but seen in its reflected light.[28]

Whatever the conscious conceptual influence of Frank's photographs, there is something in *L.A. Confidential* that corresponds to Szarkowski's notion of equivocating indirection, namely in Hanson's shift away from barbarism to those who endure in its wake. More lamentation than howl, his film lacks the feverish aspect of Ellroy's novel principally because of the way in which the story's violence is attenuated. There's no question that it would have been difficult for Hanson to shoot the novel as written, but there is something deeper at work here than censorship.

When *L.A. Confidential* was released, much attention was given to the fidelity with which Hanson and Helgeland had adapted the novel. More significant still are the ways in which the screenplay and the direction moved the story away from the novelist and his dark places. Ellroy painted a picture of the darkest noir, which was the truth as he saw it. For Hanson, the truth of Los Angeles isn't only located in its courtrooms, police precincts and brothels but in the contradictions of its iconography, in the differences between the sun-blasted days and the desert-chilled nights, between a glamorous Hurrell fantasy and a Weegee crime scene. His Los Angeles is a city of shadows but it is also a place of light, beauty and possibility, even if there are times when much of that light, beauty and possibility seems to exist only on a movie screen. His *L.A. Confidential* may be steeped in nostalgia but the longing is less for a city or a time past than for the movies as they were – larger and better than life, irresistible. By filtering the story through the movies, Hanson could remain faithful to Ellroy's novel and to his own identity as a director, as an Angeleno who never left the city and, crucially, as a lover of Hollywood history and keeper of its flame.

Curtis Hanson should have been born in Los Angeles, but his parents were in Reno, Nevada, when he came into the picture on 24 March 1945. Mother Beverly June and father Wilbur had grown up in Los Angeles and met while attending Hollywood High School. A schoolteacher, Wilbur had been a conscientious objector during the Second World War, and had been sent by the federal government to work on a construction crew in Reno, which is why his son missed being a native Angeleno. Less than a year later, the family returned to Los Angeles, settling into a neighbourhood then known as the Wiltern area, less than a mile from where James Ellroy would later move in with his father. (Hanson's father resumed teaching on his return to L.A., first at an elite high school where no less than Fox studio chief Daryl F. Zanuck had him kicked out for being a conscientious objector.) As children, Curtis Hanson and James Ellroy each separately rode their bicycles in and around their neighbourhoods, and there's a chance the two boys, just three years apart in age, might have crossed paths if the Hansons hadn't subsequently moved to Reseda, a small community tucked into the San Fernando Valley. A swath of flatlands edged by mountains, the Valley of the 1950s was mostly farmland with acre upon acre of citrus groves and, in many crucial respects, worlds apart from the rest of Los Angeles. As a child, Hanson would be dropped off to stay with his fraternal grandparents in Hollywood; later, the teenager would hitchhike to visit his uncle's family in Beverly Hills, itself a world apart from L.A.

In the 1950s, the future director's uncle, Jack Hanson, owned a successful Beverly Hills clothing store called Jax. Curtis, immersed in movie love, had dropped out of high school at the age of seventeen with the idea of somehow breaking into film-making, and for a short time he worked at his uncle's store selling women's shoes. Given the location, the clientele and even the sales clerks, Jax wasn't all that far removed from the promise of Hollywood. 'Jack was an avid movie fan and his customers were movie people', said Hanson,

What the store was famous for were the Jax Pants, which were worn by people like Audrey Hepburn and Marilyn Monroe. They were distinctive because they were cut to the woman's body and so skinny women like Hepburn loved them. In fact, when they made the TV series, *Peter Gunn*, Jax clothes were what Lola Albright wore. Dean Martin's daughters worked in the store; Sinatra's daughters worked in the store. Beverly Hills was a small town at that time. There were a couple restaurants – La Scala and the Luau – and lots of people knew one another.[28]

The fan and the businessman bought into a small, struggling movie magazine called *Cinema*. One of the few of its kind in the United States at

A page from *Cinema*, 1966

that time, the bi-monthly magazine published serious articles about movies written by serious writers, including aspiring film-maker Peter Bogdanovich. (Under Hanson's stewardship, contributors included screenwriter Robert Towne and science fiction author Harlan Ellison.) If it wasn't on an intellectual par with the likes of *Film Culture*, the landmark New York periodical in which Andrew Sarris had published his historic 'Notes on the Auteur Theory', the magazine was nonetheless proof that Los Angeles' native movie culture had begun to take root. Still, Jack Hanson's aspirations for the magazine were initially fairly downmarket: he wanted to run advertisements in the magazine that would plug his store and editorial stories that would show his well-heeled customers wearing his clothes. When he and the magazine's founder, Jim Silke, parted company, Hanson's nephew, then nineteen, convinced his uncle to let him try and put out an issue himself. It was 1964.

'My first interview', said Curtis Hanson,

was with Dalton Trumbo, which shows you where my head was. My interest in doing the magazine was to talk about movies with the people who made them, people who, it seemed to me, were happy to have somebody interested and knowledgeable about their stuff. I interviewed people whose work I admired, which in many cases meant they were inactive. I wrote very few reviews. Mainly I did interviews and a lot of photography. I went from borrowing a camera for the first issue to taking almost all of the pictures and doing the art direction. I would go around to the studios and order from their crew sheets, which was another great way to learn photography. It's what made me comfortable with the movie camera – just looking, ordering and cropping.[30]

Hanson ran *Cinema* for about three years, before venturing into the movie industry, where his trajectory over the next three decades followed a familiar arc. His first professional screenwriting gig (and first screen credit, under his full name Curtis Lee Hanson) was the 1970 genre film *The Dunwich Horror*, for American International Pictures. That film's executive producer Roger Corman subsequently co-financed and distributed Hanson's directorial feature debut, a movie with former teen idol Tab Hunter called *Sweet Kill* (later renamed *The Arousers*), about an impotent California gym teacher with a mother fixation. The film received charitable notices and Hanson kept at it. Over the next few decades, he worked on projects that fell apart, finished films for other directors and evinced a gift for untested young talent, giving Tom Cruise, for instance, one of his first major roles in a movie called *Losin' It.* Hanson wrote and directed a crypto-Hitchcock suspenser called *The Bedroom Window*, and with his friend and mentor, Samuel Fuller, wrote the screenplay for *White Dog*, a controversial film directed by Fuller about a white German Shepherd raised to attack black people. The eccentric exception to Hanson's genre output was his fine (co-written) screenplay for *Never Cry Wolf*, based on the book by Canadian naturalist Farley Mowat.

'As a writer, I was extremely selective in what I wrote,' said Hanson. 'I was writing what I loved. As a director, on the other hand, I was sort of scrambling to just get the opportunity to direct, because the world of independent film as it exists today wasn't there.'[31] Between nurturing stories he cared about and grabbing what work he could, Hanson began to make a name for himself in thrillers. To an extent, he was simply helping to fill a demand, as Hollywood in the 1980s and early 90s became increasingly enamoured with action, spectacle and the big-bang theory of the blockbuster. It's a period of American film that many consider the nadir of recent Hollywood history, but it was a climate that proved favourable to Hanson, who shared with Fuller a gift for narrative economy, a sense of the medium's moral imperative and a killer instinct for grabbing audiences by the throat. Beginning in 1990, Hanson wrote and directed a string of profitable features – *Bad Influence*, *The Hand That Rocks the Cradle* and *The River Wild* – that attracted mounting critical attention. The films were 'high-concept', in the sense that they could be bought and sold in one sentence, but in their technical craft and professionalism they were unequivocally grounded in the classic Hollywood tradition. *The River Wild* wasn't just a thriller with Meryl Streep; it was Hanson's Anthony Mann Western.

It was also the box-office success that provided Hanson the leverage he needed to make the film he wanted. In 1990, producer David L. Wolper, who then had a deal with Warner Bros., had bought the rights to *L.A. Confidential* with the hopes of turning it into a television mini-series.[32] Nothing came of it. A few years later, Hanson read Ellroy's novel for pleasure and responded to it immediately:

I thought, this is the L.A. story that I want to tell because it's the L.A. of my childhood. I'd always wanted to try and deal with the difference between appearance and reality in Los Angeles, the city of manufactured dreams. It was clearly going to be a mammoth undertaking to get a script out of this and my thought was, 'I'll option the book and figure it out on my own over however long it takes.'[33]

He then approached Wolper and Warner Bros. executive Bill Gerber, both of whom were intrigued by the idea of Hanson directing but wanted him to commit to finishing a script before making another film. Unwilling to do so, he went off to direct *The River Wild*.

'I kept thinking, floating around on the river, about these characters, you know, and L.A.,' Hanson recalled. 'The minute I got back, I met with them again and said okay.'[34] Meanwhile, Helgeland, whose credits included the thriller *Highway to Hell*, had been trying to persuade Warner Bros. to let him have a shot at the Ellroy adaptation. When he learned that Hanson had been signed to write and direct, he contacted him and, after one meeting, the two became writing partners. Although Hanson had a deal with Warner Bros., no one at the studio was interested in producing a dark, difficult period piece without easily recognisable heroes. It was at this point that Bill Gerber, the Warner executive in charge of the project, manoeuvred the project over to New Regency, one of the more adventurous production companies on the studio's lot. Run by Arnon Milchan, a former gun-runner turned art-house patron of films such as *Once Upon a Time in America* and *Brazil*, New Regency had the money and the muscle Hanson needed.

'I met Arnon before he read the script,' said Hanson.

Hanson's pitch portfolio

I had prepared a group of photographs I felt represented what the movie would ultimately be. There was a Weegee, a crime shot. There were images of Los Angeles, a particularly salacious cover of *Confidential* magazine. I'd say, 'Okay, that's the image – now peel it back and we get to *L.A. Confidential*, where our characters live.' There were a couple of Bill Claxton photos of jazz musicians, Gerry Mulligan and Chet Baker. I said, 'Look what these guys look like. They're cool, they're hip. And this is what the movie will sound like, it will be their music.' I wanted to make the point that this was not going to be *The Big Sleep*, it was not going to be an homage to Chandler's world of the 1930s and 1940s – it was the forward-looking 1950s, which is still very much with us.

I had a couple of publicity shots of actors, of Aldo Ray, and I said, 'This is what Bud White's going to look like, if I could cast it out of show-business heaven.' There was a shot of Guy Madison and I said, 'This is what Jack Vincennes is going to look like; a clotheshorse, wearing clothes we would all love to wear and our girlfriends would love to see us in.' I had a couple of Hurrell-type photos of movie stars, and said, 'This is what the movie isn't, except when Kim Basinger is selling to the suckers. This is what she's pretending to be.' There was a great shot of Veronica Lake. I went through this with Arnon, discussing the theme and explaining the characters, and how with each of the characters and also with the city of L.A., it appears to be one thing but is something else. And when I finished, Arnon said, 'Let's make the movie.'[35]

3 Whatever You Desire

With the Nite Owl massacre, *L.A. Confidential* shifts to a different register, as does our sense of what is at stake in this chaos. The air of everyday barbarism – from Bud's assault on the wife-beater to the bandages on Susan Lefferts's face, the blithe manner in which the dreams of the dope-smoking actors are extinguished and the eagerness with which the police pummel the Mexican prisoners – begins to assume a terrible weight. In scene after scene, the battered and bruised accumulate, creating a stockpile of casualties, which makes the Nite Owl – a very ordinary coffee shop turned extraordinary charnel house – seem inevitable. This inevitability parallels Ellroy's determinism but there is, at least in the film, an instrumental aspect to the carnage: the murders kick-start the plot, give the detectives something to do and justify the way in which they go about their vengeful business. At the downtown division, Dudley Smith convenes the department, announcing that the suspects are three young black men who, the night of the massacre, had been seen discharging shotguns while driving a maroon Mercury coupé in a local park. Ed and Jack team up to track the three black men, while Bud, having realised that one of the Nite Owl victims is Susan Lefferts, follows her trail back to Pierce Patchett.

Ed and Jack drive to the black neighbourhood of South Central, where they pump a boxer for information. He tips them off to a suspect

The bad and the beautiful: Ed and Jack in South Central

who owns a maroon coupé and likes to shoot dogs. At the suspect's home, Ed (who can't find his glasses) and Jack encounter two detectives from Smith's Mobster Squad, Breuning and Carlisle, who, having already arrived at the scene, are peering into a maroon coupé. The four detectives enter the house and arrest three black men. During the siege, Breuning yells 'Ace him, Jack,' bidding Vincennes to shoot one of the suspects; Jack doesn't but Carlisle fires his shotgun and Exley cautions them not to kill anyone. Jack suspiciously asks, 'Anxious aren't you, Carlisle?' Back at the station, Ed interrogates the detainees in separate rooms, as the rest of the division watches through one-way glass partitions. During the questioning, a suspect reveals that he and his friends have kidnapped and raped a woman, who is still being held captive. Bud bursts into the interrogation room and thrusts his gun into the suspect's mouth, demanding to know where the woman is. The suspect confesses, but only after Bud has squeezed three blank shots down his throat. At the new location, Bud secures Smith's permission to enter alone first; inside, he shoots an unarmed black man. Inez Soto is rescued.

Although Ed sneers about the murder to Bud, it is never mentioned again, an absence of moral and judicial reckoning that speaks volumes about the well-named White, the department and the city in which the death goes unnoticed. During the 1940s, thousands of Americans poured into Los Angeles looking for wartime work; many of these new arrivals were black, such as struggling writer Chester Himes, who came to the city with hopes of finding a position in Hollywood. During the three years he lived in the city, Himes held twenty-three jobs. One of those he tried and failed to secure was as a reader at Warner Bros., where he was refused work by none other than Jack Warner, who said, Himes claimed, 'I don't want no niggers on this lot.'[36] Himes did sweat it out at a couple of the area's shipyards, an experience that made its way into his scabrous 1945 novel about the city's topology of hate, *If He Hollers Let Him Go*. 'If you couldn't swing down Hollywood Boulevard and know that you belonged,' the book's hero rages,

if you couldn't make a polite pass at Lana Turner at Ciro's without having the gendarmes beat the black off you for getting out of your place; if you couldn't eat a thirty-dollar dinner at a hotel without choking on the insults, being a great big 'Mister' nigger didn't mean a thing.[37]

Of Los Angeles, Himes later said,

racism became an inescapable fact of life for me. I'd been able to ignore segregation up until then, but now I couldn't. I felt I could 'see' racism, and it seemed to stick to me. It contaminated everything. It was like a disease I couldn't shake. [38]

It is a disease no one shakes in *L.A. Confidential*. Ellroy's unnerving deployment of invective hammers this point home time and again. In the novel, blacks are 'niggers' and 'spooks'; Mexicans are 'taco benders'; Italians are 'wops'; Jews are 'hebes'. Women are 'quiff' and 'gash'. Ellroy's

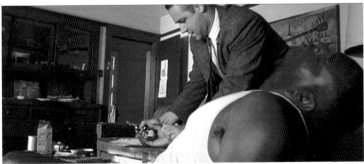

Bud terrifies a witness; and plants evidence

calculating insults can be shocking but are of a splenetic piece with a splenetic milieu; however repugnant, the words mostly sound true when spat from the mouths of the (mostly) white men who voice them. It's instructive, though, that Ellroy's crudest vituperation doesn't make it into the film. Arguably the most fractious word in the United States, 'nigger', is never uttered, though the cops do call Mexicans 'spics'. Part of this is purely strategic. In purging Ellroy's language, particularly the slurs against blacks, Hanson and Helgeland acknowledge that while American audiences will tolerate black characters calling one another 'nigger' in specific contexts, they are less comfortable when the words are spoken by white characters, even in period drag.

By cleaning up Ellroy's language, the screenwriters also clean up their three detectives. In the novel, Smith has stolen Mickey Cohen's heroin with the intention of pumping it into black neighbourhoods. During the book's delirious conclusion, Bud unravels the captain's motivation for Ed and Jack, echoing the sort of conspiracy theories that periodically makes the American alternative-political rounds: 'Dud was talking up his containment shit, and he said something about keeping the niggers sedated, which sounds like heroin to me.' Smith's strategy for tranquillising the black population doesn't prick the moral outrage of the detectives, who in Ellroy's original are far uglier in deed and motivation. In the book, Jack isn't just on the take: he is a recovering addict and alcoholic who, while doped up, mortally wounded two innocent bystanders. Bud's acts of grotesque savagery include shoving a man's hand down a garbage disposal until the fingers are chewed to the bone; he also bites a man's nose off and steps on another one's face until his victim stops breathing. Ed, for his part, lives with the knowledge that the Second World War medal he took home was given to a coward who hid from the enemy. In Ellroy's world the living only seem better off than the dead.

As with the framed black suspects, Patchett the pimp, his various prostitutes and the *Hush-Hush* hobgoblin, the detectives themselves constitute part of the film's larger, 'confidential' story, embodiments of the trouble in paradise referred to by Hudgens in the opening montage. Just as the black suspects pull the detectives into a Los Angeles rarely represented in period films of the 1950s, opening a window onto the city's race relations, Lynn, Patchett, Susan Lefferts and Matt Reynolds (one of the actors arrested during Jack's Hollywood Pot Bust) tug the story into the equally opaque world of high-end prostitution. While Ed and Jack are out looking for the black suspects, Bud has driven to Patchett's Hollywood Hills mansion, believing that the pimp may be able to provide information about Stensland and Susan Lefferts, and what the two were doing together at the Nite Owl the night they were murdered. Although Patchett denies knowing anything about the massacre, he volunteers the information that he peddles women who either look like movie stars or undergo surgery to augment the resemblance. 'I needed a Rita Hayworth to fill out my little studio,' he says of Lefferts. 'There's Gardner, Russell, Monroe, Turner. Lynn Bracken is my Veronica Lake.'

In his memoirs, screenwriter Budd Schulberg, the son of the early prominent studio executive, B. P. Schulberg, wrote about landing in Los Angeles with his family in 1918 and staying at the Alexandria Hotel, where male guests paid to enjoy the services of sham starlets:

A generation later there was to be a famous bordello in Hollywood … There you could find look-alikes for Carole Lombard, Jean Harlow, Claudette Colbert, and Nancy Carroll. But the later clientele was indulging in fantasies while the greenhorns in the throbbing lobby of the Alexandria, living in simpler times, really believed they were achieving an immortal roll in the hay with Bebe Daniels or Alice Joyce.[39]

In *L.A. Confidential*, prostitutes look like movie stars and movie stars look like prostitutes, because it can be hard to tell the difference in a movie-made city like Los Angeles, where reality and fantasy continually eclipse each other. (Patchett even calls Ed and Jack 'celebrity' policemen.) As British architecture critic Reyner Banham once wrote,

Visiting houses in Beverly Hills or Bel Air can be an hallucinating experience; an overwhelming sense of déjà vu mingles with an overwhelming desire to sidle along corridors with one's back to the wall and to kick doors wide open before passing through.[40]

Spend a week in L.A. and it's easy to see what Banham meant. The déjà vu is overwhelming, at times bewildering. Notwithstanding the recent crisis of runaway production, the city has long proved a favourite backlot for innumerable films, television programmes, commercials and music videos. During its Golden Age, Paramount employed a location map that reflected the region's geological diversity by fancifully dividing Southern California into the likes of 'the Swiss Alps', 'Sherwood Forest, England', and 'the Sahara Desert'. In much the way that the map comprised a virtual country, most of the key locations in L.A. Confidential comprise something of a virtual city, a vision of Los Angeles as an instantly urban, noir-inflected metropolis, one bearing little relationship to the growing, post-war suburban sprawl. With few exceptions, such as the suburban home in Bud's first scene, most of the story unfolds in and around Hollywood and downtown, two of the city's more storied neighbourhoods and home to the police stations in which the detectives are stationed. Hollywood is the site of one drug bust, two executions and three bars, as well as Hudgens's office, the Badge of Honor set and the liquor store in which Bud meets Lynn. Downtown and its periphery are where the Nite Owl massacre occurs, where the black suspects escape to and where Mrs Lefferts mourns her daughter in the misleadingly bucolic sounding Elysian Park (now the site of much LAPD training). This isn't the suburbs or the sprawl; this is Los Angeles as City, as New York City, as Chicago – anywhere but here.

The movies have perennially remade Los Angeles into its fantasy image, and for as long as films have been shot in the city Angelenos have approved and refused that image. When Schulberg moved to the city in 1918, he found that 'although the Great War had broken down some of the resistance to movie people "No movies" was still a sign to be found in many a boardinghouse window on the quiet streets of Hollywood.'[41] In 1910, Los Angeles' population had been 319,198; forty years later, it was almost two million.[42] By the time the Second World War ended, the very landscape was being reshaped and re-imagined, from the newly built freeway system to the Case Study Houses, single-family homes designed with an eye toward the new age. Even so, by the early 1950s, the Los Angeles of the Future was still a work in progress, part suburb, part citrus grove, and would remain so for decades. It wasn't all that long ago that the notion of something like 'Los Angeles culture' was deemed an oxymoron; in some quarters it still is. (In the 1978 film of his play, *California Suite*, Neil Simon dubbed the city 'paradise with a lobotomy'.) What Los Angeles did have by way of culture were the movies, which not only helped build its economy but also changed its geography, its architecture and its gestalt.

To gauge the influence of the film industry on Los Angeles it's important to remember when the motion pictures arrived. 'Lacking socially prominent first families or deeply rooted social traditions,' social historian Carey. McWilliams wrote in 1946, 'Los Angeles quickly adopted the motion-picture elite as its arbiters of taste and style … In other words, Los Angeles imitated Hollywood.'[43] Yet by the time that Los Angeles was reaching its majority, as it were, Hollywood seemed be slipping into obsolescence. 'Hollywood's like Egypt. Full of crumbled pyramids,' producer David O. Selznick said to screenwriter Ben Hecht in 1951. 'It'll never come back. It'll just keep on crumbling until finally the wind blows the last studio prop across the sands.'[44] During the early 1950s, the industry was doing more than just crumbling – it was collapsing. As the number of televisions in American homes multiplied, movie attendance went into precipitous decline; in 1951, an estimated fifty-four million people attended the movies on a weekly basis, down from the ninety million of three years earlier. That same year, the House Committee on Un-American Activities held its second hearing, feeding the blacklist and the movie industry's fear. It had been three years since the 1948 *Paramount* anti-trust decree, which, along with the incursion of television into American homes, seemed to be destroying the studio system that Selznick, Hecht and B. P. Schulberg had helped build.

Traces of decadent, crumbling Hollywood are everywhere in L.A. Confidential – on marquees for *When Worlds Collide* and Vincente

Minnelli's *The Bad and the Beautiful*, a 1952 release that stars one of *L.A. Confidential*'s minor characters, Lana Turner. There's a little Hollywood in the city's more quotidian corners, too, in watering holes such as the Formosa Cafe, where Bud squeezes information out of Johnny Stompanato by squeezing the snitch's testes, the same restaurant-bar in which Ed later mistakes the 'real' Turner for one of Patchett's prostitutes. But Hollywood is more than just letters on a marquee; it is an idea, an ideal, a hope and a promise. It is, film critic Otis Ferguson wrote, 'a state of mind', though he did jokingly wondering whose. The jab is the sort that guarantees laughs in New York but it discounts the humanity behind the clichés. Jack, nicknamed 'Hollywood Jack', works for television and teaches a cop how to walk and talk like him, the irony being that the detective learned his smoother moves from the movies, the very industry that TV is fast helping put out of business. Lynn makes her living from her resemblance to Veronica Lake, a 1940s star who was already a has-been by the early 1950s. The first time Bud shows up at her door, Lynn is servicing a middle-age john, who, with some tough-guy bravado lifted from the movie unwinding in the living room, asks if she would like him to get rid of the interloper. As Lake purrs onscreen in *This Gun for Hire*, Bud flashes his badge to the would-be Alan Ladd. 'LAPD, shitbird. Get the fuck out of here or I'll call your wife to come get you.'

At first, Bud and Lynn stick to a script they've likely uttered countless times before, with attitude copped from Ladd and Lake, Bogart and Bacall. As nurses a glasse of scotch, he thrusts ('you fuck for money'), she parries ('There's blood on your shirt. Is that an integral part of your job?'). When he brings up Lefferts, Lynn explains how working for Patchett allows her and others like her to hold on to their dreams. 'Sue came on a bus with dreams of Hollywood and this is how they turned out. Thanks to Pierce, we still get to act a little.'[45] With platinum hair more guarded then peek-a-boo, the then-42-year-old Basinger looks nothing like Lake, who was half her age at the height of her popularity. That difference in years, as well as the regret in Basinger's voice, deepens the sadness of the words. For some, there isn't much difference between working for Patchett or trying to make it in the movies: either way you're screwed. It's a theme Hanson and

Helgeland weave through the film, eventually tightening it around contract player Matt Reynolds. While Bud pines for Lynn, Jack is reinstated as the *Badge of Honor* technical adviser, which brings Hudgens sniffing around. The reporter explains to Jack that he's paying Reynolds to sleep with District Attorney Ellis Loew for a *Hush-Hush* sting, sealing the deal by promising the now-broke actor a gig on the show. But Reynolds ends up with his throat slashed, his dream become a nightmare.

In 1921, the Hollywood Chamber of Commerce published an advertisement that warned:

Don't Try To Break into the Movies in Hollywood Until You Have Obtained <u>Full, Frank and Dependable Information</u> from the Hollywood Chamber of Commerce. It May Save Disappointments. Out of 100,000 Persons Who Started at the Bottom of the Screen's Ladder of Fame Only Five Reached the Top.[46]

Lynn on Christmas Eve; and with Veronica Lake

Less than two decades later, Hollywood was no longer a neighbourhood trying to fend off the advancing hordes; it had become 'the world's great bullshit center' (John Dos Passos), 'a dream dump' (Nathanael West), 'a mining town in lotus land' (F. Scott Fitzgerald).[47] Los Angeles had swallowed Hollywood and was eaten in return: the movie companies begot the company town. To the outside world, it didn't matter where one began and the other left off. To those who had bought the image, then suffered its indignities, such as Chester Himes, it mattered a great deal. It may have been a fiction but it was still a place where people lived and died. 'To a sizable bulk of our population,' Ferguson wrote in 1941, 'Hollywood is where you go when you die, if you're good. To some of our more impatient critics, Hollywood is where you die if you go there.'[48] 'When I came out to L.A. this isn't exactly where I saw myself ending up,' Matt Reynolds says to Jack, shortly before he ends up dead, his blood draining into a motel carpet. Says Jack, 'Yeah, well, get in line.'

Another bad Hollywood ending

4 Men at War

Of course it ends badly. There is the unarmed black man, eating cereal and watching cartoons while dressed in his BVDs as police swarm outside. Bud shoots him, planting a gun in his cooling hand. As Inez Soto is being rescued, her rapists, the three black men who have been wrongly arrested for the Nite Owl massacre, escape from the downtown precinct. Returning to the station, Ed and one of Smith's goons, Carlisle, follow a tip to Bunker Hill, a ruin of a neighbourhood that had been a picturesque crime scene for decades. Inside a dilapidated Victorian building, Ed and Carlisle, armed with shotguns, make their way down a hallway as Exley frantically pats a front pocket; again he's looking for his glasses and again can't find them. Bursting into the room, the cops come face to face with the escaped prisoners in the company of a fourth man. As the men raise their hands, a beer bottle falls to the floor and shatters. Carlisle shoots one of the men and is shot by another in turn. Ed shoots the shooter. Another man yells, pulls out a revolver and is met with a shotgun blast from Ed as the third and remaining escapee runs from the apartment. With Carlisle's blood splattered across his face, Ed races through an adjacent apartment down a hall to the elevator, where he fires on the last man. Back at the station, he is renamed 'Shotgun Ed' by a camaraderie of back-slapping detectives. Baptised in blood, he is now one of them.

Ed shoots to kill

With the black suspects dead the Nite Owl case is officially closed. Exley's baptism launches an intermezzo of sorts comprised of seven brief scenes keyed to jazz singer Kay Starr's 1952 hit, 'Wheel of Fortune'. Although the scenes contain diegetic sound and a few freighted lines of dialogue, the 3 minute, 22 second song, with its plaintive tone and lyrics, drives the sequence. Ed is awarded the Medal of Valor for shooting the escapees; Jack returns to the *Badge of Honor* set. Bud watches Lynn's house while seated in his car – alone, in the dark, in the rain – as Starr sings 'I'll be yearning, yearning'. The would-be Alan Ladd, a city councilman, is confronted with photographs of him with Lynn and changes his vote at a meeting. Patchett smiles at a ribbon-cutting ceremony marking the opening of the Santa Monica Freeway as a voice booms, 'Go West America was the slogan of Manifest Destiny, today is that last step westward.' There's a Fleur-

'Shirley Temple' plays with her john; and Lynn tames her wolf

de-Lis bacchanal at which two women dance together while a Shirley Temple lookalike dangles on a geezer's knee and Lynn trades glances with Patchett. Last, Bud uneasily watches another of Smith's goons pummel a hood as the captain issues a caution, 'Go back to Jersey, sonny. This is the City of the Angels and you haven't got any wings.'

Hanson and Helgeland have distilled the essentials: Ed has been accepted into the police fold, Jack has returned to *Badge of Honor* and Bud is miserable, whether he's pining or pounding. In the next, far longer section (twenty-one scenes), the developments of the intermezzo pay off, with each detective facing down the man he has become – coward, mercenary, thug – and, through another, transforming himself into the man he could or should be. For Bud, the agent of change is Lynn, a woman who, because she can save herself (she's moving back home to open a dress shop) doesn't need him as her rescuer. Freed of that burden, and hoping to get out of Dudley Smith's Mobster Squad by proving his intelligence, Bud initiates his own private investigation into the Nite Owl. His inquiry leads him beneath Mrs Lefferts' house, where he finds the decomposed corpse of Leland 'Buzz' Meeks and wonders how and why it got there. Jack, meanwhile, runs into Hudgens squiring Reynolds on the *Badge of Honor* set and learns of the reporter's plan to trap District Attorney Loew in headline-screaming flagrante delicto. This isn't the Los Angeles life that Reynolds had in mind but, with Hudgens and Jack's encouragement, he makes a move on Loew, having been promised money

Mrs. Lefferts in Elysian Park

and a spot on the television programme for his efforts. Hudgens sneers at the actor's naiveté and while Jack looks embarrassed by the deal, he nonetheless pockets his payoff.

There's an air of melancholy and escalating urgency throughout these scenes. When Bud and Lynn take in a screening of *Roman Holiday* he doesn't look at Audrey Hepburn but gazes intently at the woman next to him. When, after leaving Hudgens, Jack sits in a tavern called the Frolic Room, he's similarly distracted and his thoughts seem similarly elsewhere. Once again, the soundtrack for his life comes courtesy of Dean Martin, who this time is crooning his insipidly upbeat cover of 'Powder Your Face with Sunshine'. As 'Hollywood Jack' sits at the bar listening to Dino's pickled brio ('the future's brighter when hearts are lighter, so smile smile smile'), he stares down at the $50 bill Hudgens gave him. Lifting his eyes, Jack takes in his own mirrored reflection staring across at him, hard and unsmiling. Abruptly he leaves the Frolic Room, the bill stretched over his glass of whisky, and drives to the motel where Hudgens instructed Reynolds to meet Loew. Although Jack is early for the assignation he's not early enough: Reynolds is dead and the District Attorney is nowhere to be seen. Stunned, Jack shakes his head, registering a kind of tender despair in a face that only now has taken the full measure of its reflection.

Reynolds's death induces Jack to work with Ed, a man he's thus far given no quarter. Exley, troubled by the deaths of the men he shot, begins

Jack at the Frolic Room

to wonder if something is wrong with the now-closed Nite Owl case. Sitting in the downtown bureau, he tells Jack the story of 'Rollo Tomasi', a name he gave the anonymous gunman who killed his father. 'It was supposed to be about justice,' says Ed, before asking Jack why he became a cop. Vincennes quietly answers: 'I don't remember.' Until now, each of the three detectives has pursued distinctly separate directions. Ed has followed the Nite Owl to the black suspects only to discover that Inez Soto has lied about the time frame of her rape and that the men are figuratively as well as literally a dead end. (Her reasons for lying – she's Latina and poor, and no one would otherwise listen – are pure Ellroy: 'I did what I had to do for justice.') Bud, meanwhile, has chased his dead partner's trail from the massacre to Patchett, Lynn, Mrs Lefferts and Buzz Meeks. After helping capture the Nite Owl suspects, Jack has travelled a different route that has taken him from the Fleur-de-Lis business card to the arty porn and, ultimately, to Reynolds. Now, when Ed solicits his help in re-investigating the Nite Owl, Jack agrees on the condition that Exley help with the young actor's murder, 'another Hollywood homo-cide' that no one else cares about.

In his taxonomy of detective fiction, literary theorist Tzvetan Todorov wrote that in the thriller 'everything is possible, and the detective risks his health, if not his life'.[49] It is true that everything is possible in the thriller; 'everything', however, is rarely ventured. In its serial form, the detective's life hinges on the continuing success of the franchise. This brute commercial fact is all the more inescapable when it comes to the Hollywood thriller, which is equally dependent on suspense (what happens) and familiarity (nothing too extreme or foreign). In 'the story of the vulnerable detective,' wrote Todorov, 'the detective loses his immunity, gets beaten up, badly hurt, constantly risks his life, in short, he is integrated into the universe of the other characters, instead of being an independent observer as the reader is.'[50] For Todorov, vulnerability helps sustain the reader's 'expectation of what will happen', thereby creating suspense. But in the Hollywood thriller, suspense is diminished by our familiarity with the unwritten industry rule that if the detective is the lead character he must not die, especially if he's a star. Those who die in thrillers are sacrificial, like the cordons of fallen police whose deaths establish the need for the heroic individualism of the solitary cop.

There are so few exceptions to the invulnerable detective that when Jack is shot through the heart while seated in Smith's kitchen the shock of his death reverberates long after the scene ends. Hollywood of the early and mid-1990s was not a place of great expectations or surprises, and the death of a lead character, especially one played by the actor who had top billing, was genuinely surprising. This was a period of formulaic spectacular action-adventures with cartoon-like heroes who bounced back from every blow as if they were punching bags, armed with as many fast quips as guns. Having started off with the mocking inflections of Hudgens's introductory narration, *L.A. Confidential* has quickly become nothing if not serious; by the time of the Nite Owl, its Los Angeles sun has entered a near total eclipse. Throughout the fade to noir, Jerry Goldsmith's mournful horns and rumbling drums are interspersed with period songs that veer from big-band brass to cool jazz from the likes of Chet Baker and Gerry Mulligan, and which often work an ironic counterpoint to the images on screen. One of the last songs in the film, in fact, is 'Powder Your Face with Sunshine', the horror of which only becomes apparent with Jack's murder. As he sits in Smith's kitchen, it is the very banality of the scene – the household bric-a-brac, Dudley's pyjamas and tartan bathrobe, even his lilting offer of a cup of tea – that raises Jack's murder to the level of tragedy.

The face powdered with sunshine has become a death mask. Spacey deepens the transformation by shedding the character's bonhomie to reveal the man underneath. Not yet a Hollywood star, the actor had received top billing after enjoying a run playing first-rate creeps in films such as *The Usual Suspects*, for which he won an Academy Award. At the time he was still considered more of a character actor and perhaps because he is not carrying the film he is superb, a font of quicksilver emotion, never more so than after Smith shoots Jack and asks, 'Have you a valediction, boy-o?' Spacey smiles slightly, turning Jack's amusement inward with a faraway look, and utters the name 'Rollo Tomasi'. The name is a code and a gift, for when Smith later asks Ed if he's ever heard the

peculiar name, the captain has tipped his crooked hand. Smith doesn't realise it then, but Jack, by helping push Ed toward the truth, has given himself a memorable exit. He has, after straddling the LAPD and show business, and getting lost in the shuffle, managed to transcend his past and redeem himself as a man and as a cop. (This humanist gesture belongs to Hanson and Helgeland; in the novel, Jack dies an agonising death with no redemption.) As with the Nite Owl massacre, Jack's death raises the stakes in the film by becoming the excuse, the rationale and the *raison d'être* for the blood that's still to flow.

Blood is almost all that remains. ('Film noir is a film of death, in all senses of the word,' Raymond Borde and Etienne Chaumeton wrote in their 1955 *A Panorama of American Film Noir*.[51]) Shortly after Jack's murder, Hudgens dies, beaten to death by Smith; then Patchett dies, having bled to death in his mansion. Eventually, it emerges that Smith is

Jack on his way to redemption

the story's villain, its architect of doom. Ed descends on the records room in the downtown division, where he discovers that Smith once worked with Meeks and Stensland. As he attempts to make sense of this information, he's interrupted by Bud, who has just discovered photographs of Lynn in a clinch with the detective lieutenant. Lynn, trying to protect Bud, has, at Patchett's urging and in front of Hudgens's camera, had sex with Ed in an attempt to frame him. What she doesn't yet know is that Smith has arranged the peep session in hope of setting Bud against Ed, who, the captain fears, is closing in on the truth. Bud, blinded with jealous rage, confronts Lynn and slaps his lover to her knees. Then he turns his fury on Ed, who in the face of Bud's wrath shrinks to the size of a hapless clerk. When Bud hurls Ed across the file room – again and again and again once more – he is rehearsing and justifying the final, concluding destruction. Ed, bounced about the room like a rubber ball, has finally become the vulnerable male body that the thriller requires.

In the logic of the thriller, the detective is propelled by a simple imperative: beat or be beaten. Often burdened with a psychic wound or two (a drinking problem, a failed marriage or, as with Ed and Bud, a haunted past), he must amass more and more wounds as the narrative unwinds. The more frequent and intense his beatings, the greater the danger and the tension: will he live, and how? In the thriller, the beating serves two functions: it slows down the action, giving 'play' to the narrative line, and it confers on the detective a new subjectivity, that of victim. In the detective story, dead bodies serve as signposts that the detective must reach before moving to the next stage of his journey. His (rarely her) search pushes the story forward, but when he's beaten, that search slows down – without ever stopping – the momentum of the narrative. In this sense, the beatings are interludes of spectacle, like song-and-dance numbers in musicals, and as in the musical, they have a subtextual function. Much as an Astaire and Rogers dance number serves as a metaphor for the sexual congress the couple can never have, the detective's beating functions as a metaphor for the death that must never happen if the story is to continue. The detectives who don't die become victims nevertheless, either by proxy (the murdered wife is a favourite excuse) or through physical suffering. With each blow the detective is brought closer to death, which, in turn, justifies first his vengeance, then his absolution.

Invariably, the beating brings male characters closer by dividing them into victim and victimiser, executed and executor, bonding them in a

Hudgens peeps at Lynn and Ed; Smith silences Hudgens; and Ed and Bud find Patchett dead

brotherhood of blood. For Bud and Ed, that brotherhood will be sealed during an exchange of violence that has a distinctly sexual cast notably absent from the novel. When, in an earlier scene, Ed visits Lynn at her apartment to question her, only to forcibly grab and kiss her, she says,

Bud beats Lynn and Ed

'Fucking me and fucking Bud aren't the same thing.'[52] She's right. Ed won't be able to 'fuck' Bud, literally or figuratively, but her words hang over the two men as both a threat and a promise. Directly after Bud beats Lynn, he beats Ed. To an extent, he beats Ed for his sins – for the sins of the coward, for the sins of the informant, maybe even the sins of the near-sighted, though more for the sins of the man who thought he could serve justice by conforming to the rules. Bud also beats Ed because violence is also how men bond in movies of this sort; it is the language that they speak, it is the love that they dare name. It is a frisson of homoeroticism familiar from so many male-driven narratives, one that has little to do with men and love, and everything to do with the material absence of women and the killing ways in which men are forced into intimacy.

After the beating, Ed and Bud descend on Ellis Loew, hang him upside down out of his office window (a spasm of a violence worthy of Hanson's mentor Sam Fuller), and extract enough information to tighten the noose around Smith. As Ed tends to Lynn's bruises (she reads Bud's signature across his face, too), Bud learns of Hudgens's death. In one of the film's final scenes, the new partners converge at the Victory Motel, each believing that the other has summoned him to a meeting. The pair realise that they have been set up, probably by Smith, and barricade themselves in one of the motel's abandoned rooms. Lunging from wall to wall amid a storm of wood, plaster and ammunition, Bud and Ed – at last wearing his wayward glasses – are assaulted on all fronts. Slugs fly, casings

Bud plays bad cop with Loew

Gunfight at the Victory
Motel

fall. Moonlight streams between broken laths and through bullet holes pinpricking the room, illuminating the dusty churning air. The noise is deafening and the tension heart-thudding. It's a freakishly beautiful, elegantly choreographed epic of destruction: the wrecking ball is swinging hard. In Ellroy's novel, the big-bang finale sounds aboard a hijacked train (something to do with Mickey Cohen and escaped prisoners), but the bigger bang is the revelation about Ed's father and the depths of his corruption. In the film, Ed simply says, 'All I ever wanted was to measure up to my father.' Bud looks him in the eye. 'Now's your chance. He died in the line of duty, didn't he?'

The lines aren't in the book but neither is the stand-off. With the Nite Owl, the film becomes Hanson's, because it is the first scene in which the way he shoots becomes as important as what he is shooting; it is the scene in which he rises to the challenge of his material and meets it head on cinematically. From the Nite Owl massacre on, *L.A. Confidential* remains Hanson's not only because of the ways in which the plot deviates from the original text but because of the feeling and the mood he creates through lush visual pleasures rather than a mad rush of words. It's in this sense that the shoot-out at the Victory Motel becomes the apotheosis of Hanson's vision in and for the film. At this stage in the story there's precious little left of Ellroy's original narrative: Hanson and Helgeland have stripped it down to its bones. All that remains for the some seven minutes that comprise the shoot-out is sound, bodies in motion, light and dark, *mise-en-scène*. As with much of what is great in this film – Bud prowling up a flight of steps to rescue Inez Soto, Ed staring at Dudley Smith upon hearing the name Rollo Tomasi, the smile on Jack's face before he dies – the scene's power doesn't come from Ellroy's language. It comes, rather, from the film-making.

In its sheer conceptual simplicity this deus ex machina becomes an unexpected trump card for the director. Freed from Ellroy's prose, Hanson is able to bring the film to a pure cinematic climax. As such the scene becomes a reaffirmation of genre even as it also, by its very length and its useless beauty, stretches the limits of the form. Everything that Hollywood had taught Hanson seems to be poured into the shoot-out, which could have been lit by the great cinematographer John Alton but was instead lit by an Italian director of photography who, before production began, had never heard the term film noir.[53] For many directors, particularly those working in Hollywood, genre can become a prison from which they never escape. For some, it can be a liberation: American commercial cinema is by design a cinema of rebels and not of revolutionaries. Just as generations of film-makers did before them, the greatest directors working within the contemporary studio system push at film form from the inside. If, during the last several decades, the genres that were so fertile during the studios' golden age now seem exhausted, *L.A. Confidential* pays vivid testament to the ability of American cinema to, much like the country itself, regenerate through violence.[54]

It's not over. Ed is shot in the shoulder and Dudley Smith shoots Bud twice point blank. After Smith puts what seems like the last, fatal bullet in Bud, he advises Ed to join forces with him. Ed struggles to his feet and follows Smith outside. There in the Los Angeles night, with palm trees and bobbing oil pumps silhouetted against the sky, police sirens wail in the distance. Smith instructs Ed to hold up his badge 'so they'll know you're a policeman'. The corrosive irony of the line deepens when Ed shoots Dudley in the back, fatally wounding him. In that instant, Ed Exley becomes the very criminal that Smith has been for years and which, by raising his badge, the young detective will avoid being mistaken for. He raises his badge, reinforcements arrive, the scene ends. Later, in front of the police chief and district attorney, as he sits in an interrogation room behind a one-way mirror, Ed spells out the machinations by which Smith and Patchett planned to take over organized crime in Los Angeles. The chief and Loew hastily cover up Smith's death, thereby sparing the city and the LAPD scandal, and securing Ed Exley's future in the city of the future.

In the final scene, Lynn watches Ed receive another departmental medal for valour, and listens as the police chief announces that the LAPD will move into its new facilities the next year. 'Los Angeles will finally have the police force it deserves.' Lynn, whose Veronica Lake peek-a-boo has been shorn into a Marilyn Monroe bob that brings her into the 1950s,

walks with Ed to her waiting car. Swaddled in bandages, Bud sits in the
back seat nearly immobile and unable to speak, helpless as a baby. Ed
thanks Bud for 'the push' and grasps his free hand. As Jerry Goldsmith's
soundtrack loses some of its brassy edge, Lynn tells Ed that 'some men get
the world, others get ex-hookers and a trip to Arizona'. She kisses Ed, the
two say goodbye, she gets in the car and drives off. As the car pulls away,
Bud looks out the back window and waves. Ed stares back with an
expression as blank and hard as the one he wore when he entered the film.
The scene ends with a cutaway to an image of a sun-drenched Los Angeles
street, bringing the film full circle to an idyllic past that never was.[55]

Ed spins an alibi; and Bud waves goodbye to it all

Epilogue

L.A. Confidential premiered at the Cannes film festival in May 1997 and was released in the United States on 19 September of that same year. It was an immediate critical favourite. One reviewer after another offered up generous praise, deploying superlatives such as 'brilliant', 'gorgeous' and 'extraordinary'.[56] A number of writers favourably compared it to *Chinatown*, though most also felt compelled to add that it hadn't surpassed the earlier film as the ultimate in L.A. noir. Yet if the notices were ecstatic, a number of critics also sounded an unsettling note amid the adulation. Writing in *Esquire* magazine, critic David Thomson called the film a 'terrific entertainment', but worried that '*L.A. Confidential* could yet prove too demanding for big audiences – we are out of training – but there are huge narrative pleasures and swoony surprises that lift the picture off in new, darker directions.'[57] A few other reviewers agreed, with one noting the film's 'complicated' story and another referencing its 'thickets of confusion'.[58] It is a more involved narrative than can be found in most contemporary American movies, perhaps, but complication is the very meat of detective fiction, as much as stray guns and bad women. Part of the bargain we make with detective stories, after all, is that we don't always know what's going on, sometimes not until we've turned to the final page.

Although it received numerous rapturous reviews and 'performed' respectably at the box office during its lethally decisive opening weekend, the film was not an immediate success, certainly by blockbuster standards.[59] Of course, that it wasn't a blockbuster and had never been conceived as one was part of the problem. The studio releasing the film, Warner Bros., was well versed in high-concept, star-driven releases but seemed unsure how to handle a dark period piece in which the most recognisable names were two character actors and a female star on the fade. The month before, the studio had released the thriller *Conspiracy Theory*, starring Mel Gibson and Julia Roberts, from a script by Helgeland, an action movie, *Steel*, and a family movie, *Free Willy 3: The Rescue*. For Warner Bros., *L.A. Confidential* was an art movie, a categorical confusion that was born out by its release strategy. The film was previewed months in advance of its opening date, which is customary for films that are being positioned through critics and other 'word of mouth' taste-makers. In Los Angeles, a public relations firm best known for their work on independent film was hired to help co-ordinate publicity, and during the publicity rounds, Hanson and Ellroy, rather than any of the cast members, were presented as the film's stars. The film opened on 769 screens; by contrast, *Conspiracy Theory* opened on 2,806 screens, *Steel* on 1,260, *Free Willy 3* on 1,258.

Film-makers often blame marketing when their movies fare badly at the box office and Hanson did voice a few polite regrets in the press about the release after the disappointing opening. Yet it's uncertain if the film could have done much better with audiences, even with a more cogent studio strategy. By the end of 1997, numerous critics counted *L.A. Confidential* among the year's best and various critics groups had showered it with awards. The following spring it secured nine Academy Award nominations, including nods for Best Picture and Best Director, but went on to win only two awards – one for Best Screenplay (adapted) and the other for Basinger, in the Best Supporting Actress category.[60] It was routed that night by James Cameron's *Titanic*, yet another period film but one in which there was very little darkness and even less moral ambiguity. The Academy Awards are not supposed to matter to serious critics, but they should matter, because they do matter deeply in Hollywood for various material reasons, including what they augur for film-makers, for audiences and for the movies themselves. The reasons why *L.A. Confidential* failed to connect with a modern movie audience, or more to the point why the audience failed to connect with the film, remain explainable but, at last, irrational.

Notes

1 See John Fante, *Ask the Dust*, p. 12.

2 The quartet consists of *The Black Dahlia* (1987); *The Big Nowhere* (1988); *L.A. Confidential* (1990); and *White Jazz* (1992).

3 There's nothing 'natural' about Los Angeles and the orange. One of Southern California's reigning totems, the fruit was introduced into the region by the Spanish and later helped bleed dry the area's extant water supply. In his 1939 novel *Ask the Dust*, John Fante turns the totem on its head: 'The days of plenty – plenty of worries, plenty of oranges. Eat them in bed, eat them for lunch, push them down for dinner,' p. 27.

4 The timing of the premiere is off, since the film opened in 1951. Similarly, *Roman Holiday*, which Bud and Lynn take in at a theatre in what would have been early 1953, was actually released later in the year.

5 Ellroy didn't read Winchell when he was growing up, but the East Coast-based writer and his show-business inflected 'slanguage' were an overwhelming influence on low-rent journalism, and Ellroy did consume plenty of slander magazines steeped in Winchellese.

6 Hanson has said that he purposely avoided seeing the film when he cast the actor.

7 See Joe Domanick, *To Protect and To Serve: The LAPD's Century of War in the City of Dreams*, p. 111.

8 Ibid., pp. 117–34.

9 See James Ellroy, *My Dark Places*, p. 99.

10 Of the original television show *Dragnet*, which ran from 1951 to 1959, the *Hollywood Reporter* opined, 'This series is going to do more to raise the rest of the country's opinion of Los Angeles than any other show of any kind.' See Michael J. Hayde, *My Name's Friday*, p. 44.

11 See Ellroy, *My Dark Places*, p. 123. Notably, another murder recounted in *The Badge* is of a 'flaming redhead', a happily married woman who, the one night she goes out without her husband, ends up strangled to death in her car. See Jack Webb, *The Badge*, pp. 90–2.

12 See John Gilmore, *Severed*, p. 152

13 Ellroy, *My Dark Places*, p. 251.

14 See George Orwell, *Down and Out in Paris and London*, pp. 76–7.

15 See Ellroy, *My Dark Places*, p. 79.

16 Author interview, 2002.

17 See Dashiell Hammett, 'Women, Politics and Murder', in *Hammett: Crime Stories and Other Writings*, p. 211.

18 In 1956, Marcel Duhamel, the editor of Gallimard's La Série Noire, which published American-style hard-boiled detective novels, detailed the genre's requirements to novelist Chester Himes, who subsequently wrote *If He Hollers Let Him Go*. 'Get an idea. Start with action, somebody does something – a man reaches out a hand and opens a door, light shines in his eyes, a body lies on the floor, he turns, looks up and down the hall … Always action in detail. Make pictures. Like motion pictures. Always the scenes are visible. No stream of consciousness at all. We don't give a damn who's thinking what – only what they're doing. Always doing something. From one scene to another. Don't worry about making sense. That's for the end.' Quoted in James Sallis's *Chester Himes: A Life*, p. 270.

19 See Raymond Chandler, 'The Simple Art of Murder', in *Raymond Chandler: Later Novels and Other Writings*, p. 992.

20 See Edmund Wilson, 'Who Cares Who Killed Roger Ackroyd', in *Mass Culture: The Popular Arts in America*, pp. 149-53.

21 Chandler, 'The Simple Art of Murder', pp. 988–9.

22 Chandler, *The Big Sleep*, p. 4.

23 'Brian and I wanted a name that was sufficiently unusual', Hanson explained, 'that the audience would remember it from one hearing and not confuse it with any of the other multitude of names we had going. Rollo Tomasi is contrived from the names of our former pets … my dog, his cat.' Hanson, e-mail, 2003.

24 Ellroy, *L.A. Confidential*, pp. 113-14.

25 The title serves the moment nicely on several levels, not only because Lynn is about to cook her wolf, but because the late M. F. K. Fisher, Californian and food pioneer, was a woman of terrific creativity, fortitude and independence. Hanson owns the rights to Fisher's collected works.

26 Author interview, 2002.

27 Ibid. See also Eric Rudolph, 'Exposing Hollywood's Sordid Past', *American Cinematographer*, October 1997, pp. 46–7

28 See John Szarkowski, *Photography Until Now*, p. 259.

29 Author interview, 2002.

30 In 1967, a story that Hanson wrote about a set visit to Arthur Penn's *Bonnie and Clyde* prompted James Ellroy to run out and see the film as soon as it was released. 'I was 19,' said Ellroy, 'and just starting to break into houses and sniff women's undergarments in Hancock Park. There was a girl that I was obsessed with … I used to break into her house and check the medicine cabinets and steal her panties and do shit like that. And I had a key to [her brother's] little back house where he had all this stereo equipment. Like me he disdained rock and roll and was a classical music fan and unlike me he was also a film soundtrack fan. And he had a collection of *Cinema* magazine, which was just out and which was the first place that I had ever read about film directors like Samuel Fuller.' Author interview, 2002.

31 Author interview, 1997.

32 Hanson email, 2003.

33 Author interview, 1997.

34 Ibid.

35 Ibid.

36 Sallis, *Chester Himes: A Life*, p. 76.

37 See Chester Himes, *If He Hollers Let Him Go*, p. 153.

38 Sallis, *Chester Himes: A Life*, p. 77.

39 See Budd Schulberg, *Moving Pictures: Memoirs of a Hollywood Prince*, pp. 91–2.

40 See Reyner Banham, *Los Angeles: The Architecture of Four Ecologies*, p. 83.

41 Schulberg, *Moving Pictures*, p. 94.

42 See Los Angeles Almanac (www.losangelesalmanac.com).

43 See Carey McWilliams, *Southern California: An Island on the Land*, p. 345.

44 See Ben Hecht, *A Child of the Century*, p. 467.

45 This tough-poignant speech summons up familiar image of corn-fed kids stumbling onto the Boulevard, although in this case the bus ride to screen fame and fortune isn't all that long. In the book, Lefferts's mother lives in another city; in the film, as Bud discovers, she lives in the East L.A. neighbourhood of Elysian Park, an easy bus ride from Hollywood Boulevard's main drag, as well as the studios where she could have gone looking for work.

46 See Bruce Torrence, *Hollywood: The First 100 Years*, p. 88.

47 For the Dos Passos quotation see Richard Fine, *West of Eden: Writers in Hollywood 1928–1940*, p. 99; for West, see *The Day of the Locust*, p. 132; for Fitzgerald, see *The Love of the Last Tycoon*, p. 11.

48 See Otis Ferguson, *The Film Criticism of Otis Ferguson*, p. 454.

49 Our present sense of the thriller is far more elastic than that of Todorov, who places it under the rubric *série noire*. To that end, he cites Marcel Duhamel, who, in 1945, wrote of the new genre: '[we find] violence – in all its forms, and especially the most shameful – beatings, killings … Immorality is as much at home here as noble feelings … There is also love – preferably vile – violent passion, implacable hatred.' *The Poetics of Prose*, pp. 42–52.

50 Ibid., p. 51.

51 See Borde and Chaumeton, *Panorama of American Film Noir 1941–1953*, p. 5.

52 In the aftermath of 'Bloody Christmas', Jack says pretty much the same thing to Ed: 'Bud White will fuck you for this if it takes him the rest of his life.'

53 'One of the things I loved about the idea of hiring Dante Spinotti', explained Hanson, 'was that in my first conversation with him, when I said I don't want this to be approached like film noir, he said, "What's a film noir?"' Author interview, 2002.

54 I've borrowed and amended this phrase from historian Richard Slotkin's book *Regeneration Through Violence: The Mythology of the American Frontier, 1600–1860*.

55 'I wanted them driving away from city hall on the actual location,' Hanson said, 'and the only way to do it was by painting out lines on the street, removing signs, etc. We also digitally removed some background objects/buildings to return the vista to roughly what it was in 1953. I did this with one other shot in the movie, and that was the establishing shot of city hall where you see some of the city skyline.' Hanson e-mail, 2003.

56 See John Powers in (American) *Vogue* ('brilliant'); Janet Maslin in *The New York Times* ('gorgeous'); Henry Sheehan in *The Orange County Register* ('extraordinary'); all 1997.

57 See David Thomson, *Esquire*, 1997.

58 See Jay Carr in the *Boston Globe* ('complicated') and Bob Campbell in *The Star Ledger* ('thickets of confusion'), both 1997.

59 According to *Daily Variety*, the film earned $5,211,198 in its opening weekend, eventually grossing $64,616,940 in the United States. It had been originally budgeted around $40,000,000.

60 In the years since, Basinger weathered a series of flops and Helgeland supplemented his screenwriting career by directing several features. Hanson went on to direct a critically lauded adaptation of Michael Chabon's novel, *Wonder Boys*, which proved a financial disappointment. His follow-up, *8 Mile*, starring Basinger and rap singer Marshall 'Eminem' Mathers III, was both a commercial and critical success. Ellroy has published several on-line books, a collection of essays and fiction (*Crime Wave*) and another best-selling novel (*The Cold Six Thousand*). Pearce developed a cult following for his turn in the independent film *Memento*, while Spacey and Crowe have won Academy Awards for Best Actor, the former for *American Beauty*, the latter for *Gladiator*.

Credits

L.A. Confidential

USA
1997

Directed by
Curtis Hanson
Produced by
Arnon Milchan
Curtis Hanson
Michael Nathanson
Screenplay by
Brian Helgeland
Curtis Hanson
Based on the novel by
James Ellroy
Director of Photography
Dante Spinotti
Edited by
Peter Honess
Production Designer
Jeannine Oppewall
Music composed by
Jerry Goldsmith
©Monarchy Enterprises B.V.
and Regency Entertainment
(USA), Inc
Production Company
Regency Enterprises
presents
an Arnon Milchan/
David L. Wolper production
Executive Producers
David L. Wolper
Dan Kolsrud
Co-producer
Brian Helgeland
Production Accountants
Susan Montgomery
Kim Bodner

Assistant Accountant
Karen Yokomizo
Payroll Accountant
Cheryl McHugh
**Post-production
Accountant**
Marila Chappelle
Accounting Clerks
Bradley L. Gordon
Mark D. Houston
Construction Estimator
Renee Lee Alito
**Construction Accounting
Assistant**
Nancy Bullock
Production Controller
Bonnie Daniels
**Production Office
Co-ordinator**
Carolyn Crittenden
**Assistant Production
Co-ordinator**
Patti McGuire
Unit Production Manager
L. Dean Jones Jr
Location Manager
John Panzarella
**Assistant Location
Managers**
Leslie Thorson
Stephen Fischer
**Assistant to Curtis
Hanson**
Lisa Grundy
Assistant to Mr Kolsrud
Michele Platt
Assistants to Mr Milchan
Shauna Beal
Rozzana I. Ramos
Production Secretary
Sara Flamm

**Office Production
Assistant**
Dallas Taylor
**Set Production
Assistants**
John Baumhauer
Hunter Cain
Channa Paz Cajero
Jim Flowers
Tony Kountz
Jill Tharp
Kenny Vasquez
1st Assistant Directors
Linda Montanti
Drew Ann Rosenberg
2nd Assistant Director
Jim Goldthwait
**2nd 2nd Assistant
Director**
Heather Kritzer
DGA Trainee
Kevin Koster
Script Supervisors
Sharron Reynolds-Enriquez
Connie Papineau
Casting by
Mali Finn
Casting Associate
Emily Schweber
ADR Voice Casting
Barbara Harris
Extras Casting
Messenger Associates
Casting
Extras Casting Associate
Trish Stuckey
Camera Operator
Gary Jay
1st Camera Assistant
Duane 'DC' Manwiller

2nd Camera Assistant
Poly Veitzer
Camera Loader
James Apted
Key Grip
Scott Robinson
Best Boy Grip
Bob Duggan
Dolly Grip
Alberto S. Ramos
Grips
Manny Jimenez
Randy Barrett
Carlos M. Gallardo
Key Rigging Grip
Jim Duggan
Steadicam Operator
James Muro
Chief Lighting Technician
Jeffrey W. Petersen
Assistant Chief Lighting Technician
Lonnie S. Gatlin
Electricians
Cory Bibb
Jeff Durling
Nikola Ristic
Kenneth Schneider
Eric Smith
Mark Soucie
Chief Electrical Rigging Technicians
Blaise R. Dahlquist
Daryl Herzon
Still Photographers
Peter Sorel
Merrick Morton
Visual Effects Supervisor
Peter Donen
Digital Composites
The Computer Film Company

Special Effects Co-ordinators
Eric Rylander
Richard Stutsman
Special Effects
William N. Greene III
Bob King
Roger W. Lifsey
Robert Olmstead
Rudy R. Perez
David A. Schroeder
Neil Smith
1st Assistant Editor
Beth Jochem Besterveld
Assistant Editors
Michael Trent
Carole Henderson Sherr
Lightworks/Cinemaestro Assistant
Elizabeth Sherry
Main Titles Assistant Editor
Craig Kitson
Art Director
Bill Arnold
Art Department Co-ordinator
Moira Gill
Art Department Production Assistant
Andrea Morland
Set Designers
Louisa Bonnie
Julia Levine
Mark Poll
Set Decorator
Jay R. Hart
Set Decorating Buyer
Danielle M. Simpson
Lead Person
Scott Bailey
On-set Dresser
Troy Alan Peters

Swing Gang
Roger Abell
Julie Beattie-liams
Kai Blomberg
Chris Grantz
R. Patrick McGee
Doug Sieck
Storyboard Artist
Gary Thomas
Property Master
Steven B. Melton
Assistant Property Master
Al Eisenmann II
Construction Co-ordinator
Dave DeGaetano
Construction Foreman
Javier Carrillo
Construction Location Foreman
Steve Rigamai
Propmaker Foremen
Alex Carrillo
Bob Hagman
Propmakers
John C. Cales
Ralph Fierro
Tracy Fikes
Ed Galik
Head Scenic Painter
Paul J. Stanwyck
Paint Foreman
Andy Flores
Painters
Rick Broderman
Ralph Clark
Stephanie Cooney
Rod Nunnally
Alexa Shushan
Patrick Thoms
Stand-by Painter
John Hinkle

Sign Writer Supervisor
John L. Root
Sign Writer
Bruce Kerner
Labour Foreman
John K. Hill
Labourer/Tool Keeper
Michael C. Paolone
Plaster Foreman
Sal Sanchez
Head Greensman
Neil David Pontecorvo
Stand-by Greensman
Chuck Brooks
Construction Medic
Dave Krupnick
Construction Buyer
Al DeGaetano
Costumes Designed by
Ruth Myers
Costume Supervisor
Lisa Nora Lovaas
Costumers
Barry Kellogg
Gail Just
Tom MacDonald
Elizabeth Abate
Ms Basinger's Costumer
Donna O'Neal
Wardrobe Cutter/Fitter
Michael Tereschuk
Seamstress
Bella Noubarian
Make-up Supervisors
John M. Elliott Jr
Scott H. Eddo
Make-up Artists
Tommy Cole
Lance Anderson
Make-up Artist for
Ms Basinger
Francesca Tolot

Body Make-up for
Ms Basinger
Jane English
Key Hair Stylist
Janis Clark
Hairstylist
Linda Leiter Sharp
Hair Stylist for
Ms Basinger
Peter Savic
Main Titles
Pablo Ferro
Titles/Opticals
Howard Anderson
Company
Additional Titles
Title House
Colour Timer
David Orr
Trumpet Soloist
Malcolm McNab
Music Editors
Kenneth Hall
Paul Rabjohns
Music Scoring Mixer
Bruce Botnick
Soundtrack
'Ac-cent-tchu-ate the
Positive' by Johnny Mercer,
Harold Arlen, performed by
Johnny Mercer; 'Oh! Look
at Me Now' by John
DeVries, Joe Bushkin,
performed by Lee Wiley;
'Silver Bells' by Jay
Livingston, Ray Evans;
'Silent Night' by Franz
Gruber, Joseph Mohr; 'Mele
Kalikimaka' by Alex
Anderson, performed by
Bing Crosby; 'The
Christmas Blues' by Sammy
Cahn, David Holt,
performed by Dean Martin;

'Jingle Bells' by James
Pierpont; 'Look for the Silver
Lining' by Jerome Kern, Bud
DeSilva, performed by Chet
Baker; 'Hit the Road to
Dreamland' by Johnny
Mercer, Harold Arlen,
performed by Betty Hutton;
'Wheel of Fortune' by
George Weiss, Bennie
Benjamin, performed by
Kay Starr; 'Makin' Whoopee'
by Walter Donaldson, Gus
Kahn, performed by Gerry
Mulligan with Chet Baker;
'The Lady Is a Tramp' by
Richard Rodgers, Lorenz
Hart, performed by the
Gerry Mulligan Quartet;
'Powder Your Face with
Sunshine' by Carmen
Lombardo, Stanley
Rochinski, performed by
Dean Martin; 'How
Important Can It Be' by
George Weiss, Bennie
Benjamin, performed by
Joni James on *The Perry
Como Show*; 'Looking at
You' by Cole Porter,
performed by Lee Wiley; 'At
Last' by Harry Warren, Mack
Gordon, performed by Chet
Baker and the Lighthouse
All-Stars; 'But Not for Me' by
George Gershwin, Ira
Gershwin, performed by
Jackie Gleason
Soundtrack on
Restless Records
Sound Design
Terry Rodman
Roland Thai

Production Sound Mixer
Kirk Francis
Utility Sound Technician
Kay Colvin
Boom Operator
Mychal Smith
Re-recorded at
Todd-AO Studios West
Re-recording Mixers
Andy Nelson
Anna Behlmer
Supervising Sound Editor
John Leveque
Sound Editing by
SoundStorm
Assistant Sound Editor
Steven Gerrior
**Apprentice Sound
Editors**
Tim Tuchrello
Brian Best
Negative Cutter
Mo Henry
Dialogue Editors
Donald L. Warner Jr
Kimberly Lowe Voigt
Catherine M. Speakman
Mildred Iatrou
Sound Effects Recordist
Gary Blufer
Sound Effects Editors
Glenn Hoskinson
Steve Mann
Joseph DiVitale
Gordon Ecker
ADR
Recordists:
Tami Treadwell
Diane Linn
Recording Mixers:
Bob Deschaine
Charleen Richards
Supervising Editor:
Becky Sullivan

Editors:
Andrea Horta
Denise Horta
Assistant Editor:
Marc Deschaine
Foley
Artists:
John Roesch
Hilda Hodges
Supervising Editor:
Shawn Sykora
Editors:
Michael Dressel
Bob Beher
Lori Martino
Police Adviser
Call the Cops/Randy Walker
Dolby Sound Consultant
Thom 'Coach' Ehle
**Transportation
Co-ordinator**
Keith Dillin
Transportation Captain
Pete Bianco
**Transportation
Co-captains**
John Bush
James Hooks Reynolds
**Transportation
Co-captain/Mechanic**
Larry Stelling
**Transportation Office
Co-ordinator**
Mark S. DeRosa
Drivers
David W. Amberik
Richard M. Brasic
Richard Chouinard
Reed Cohan
Vince De Amicis
Russ Della
Sandra Freeman
Stephen Heinrich
Jerry Knight

Rochelle Mellon
Janet Osterman
Miles Pierno
Olin Rushin
Patsy L. Rust
Chester Sohn
Brett Stach
Charles Stepp
Steve Thompson
Dennis Yank
Kelly Yon
Gino DiVitale
Craft Services
Cajun
Ted Yonenaka
Caterer
Michelson Food Services,
Inc
Chef
Bob Lamkin
Sous Chefs
Peter Schechtal
Carlos Rodriguez
First Aid
Marie 'Ree' Hoke
Stunt Co-ordinator
Jeff Imada
Stunts
Rick Avery
Joey Box
Troy Brown
Norm Compton
Danny Costa
Richard Drown
Doc Duhame
Gary Epper
Richie Gaona
Frankie Garbutt
Bob Herron
Toby Holguin
Kevin Jackson
Fred Jin
Gene LeBell
Fred Lerner

Tom Lupo
John Meier
Jimmy Ortega
Chris Palermo
Gary Price
Robby Robinson
Troy Robinson
Danny Rogers
J. P. Romano
Jimmy Romano
Gilbert Rosales
Anthony Schmidt
Stand-ins
Joe Durrenberger
Dariea Garibaldi
Justin Petretti
Fred Scialla
Sam Whitehead
Mr Crowe's Dialect Coach
Jessica Drake
Armourer
Thell Reed
Mickey Cohen's Dog Supplied by
Studio Animal Services
Unit Publicist
Michael Battaglia
Camera Cranes and Dollies Supplied by
Chapman/Leonard Studio Equipment
Filmed with
Panavision Cameras & Lenses
Scenes from
This Gun for Hire (1942) courtesy of Universal Pictures
Roman Holiday (1953) courtesy of Paramount Pictures

Archival Footage and Photos Supplied by
AP/Wide World Photos, Archive Films, ARIQ, Bettman Archives, Budget Films, Fish Films Footage World, Fox Movietonews, Hot Shots Cool Cuts, Image Bank, National Geographic, Producers Library Service, The Roan Group, Streamline Film Archives, UCLA Film and Television Archives, Video Tape Library, WPA Film Library
Special Thanks to
The Los Angeles Conservancy, The Lovell-Health House by Richard Neutra, Bruce Loeb Security, Debbie Herrera and Vista Group, Entertainment Industry Development Corp./Los Angeles Film Office, Los Angeles Department of Water and Power, Los Angeles Department of Transportation, City of Los Angeles

Cast
Kevin Spacey
Jack Vincennes
Russell Crowe
Wendell 'Bud' White
Guy Pearce
Edmund 'Ed' Exley
James Cromwell
Captain Dudley Smith
David Strathairn
Pierce Morehouse Patchett
Kim Basinger
Lynn Margaret Bracken

Danny DeVito
Sid Hudgens
Graham Beckel
Officer Richard 'Dick' Stensland
Simon Baker Denny
Matt Reynolds
Matt McCoy
Badge of Honor star Brett Chase
Jim Metzler
City Councilman Rogers
Paul Guilfoyle
Meyer Harris 'Mickey' Cohen
Ron Rifkin
D A Ellis Loew
Paolo Seganti
Johnny Stompanato
Elisabeth Granli
Sandra Taylor
Mickey Cohen's Mambo partners
Steve Rankin
officer arresting Mickey Cohen
Allan Graf
wife-beater
Precious Chong
wife
Symba Smith
Karen, Jack's dancing partner
Bob Clendenin
Bobby, reporter at Hollywood Station
Lennie Loftin
photographer at Hollywood Station
Will Zahrn
Nick, liquor-store owner
Amber Smith
Susan Lefferts

Darrell Sandeen
Leland 'Buzz' Meeks
Michael Warwick
Chip, Sid's assistant
Shawnee Free Jones
Tammy Jordan
Matthew Allen Bretz
officer escorting Mexicans
Thomas Rosales Jr
first Mexican
Shane Dixon
Norman Howell
Brian Lally
Don Pulford
Chris Short
officers/detectives at
Hollywood Station
John Mahon
police chief
Tomas Arana
Officer Michael Breuning,
Dudley's guy
Michael McCleery
Officer William Carlisle,
Dudley's guy
George Yager
gangster at Victory Motel
Jack Conley
Vice captain
Ginger Slaughter
Ginger, secretary in Vice
Jack Knight
detective at Detective
Bureau
John H. Evans
patrolman at Nite Owl
coffee shop
Gene Wolande
forensic chief
Brian Bossetta
forensic officer
Michael Chieffo
coroner

Gwenda Deacon
Mrs Lefferts
Mike Kennedy
Bud's rejected partner
Ingo Neuhaus
Jack's rejected partner
Robert Harrison
Philip, Pierce Patchett's
bodyguard
Robert Barry Fleming
Leonard Bidwell, the boxer
Jeremiah Birkett
Sugar Ray Collins, Nite Owl
suspect
Salim Grant
Louis Fontaine, Nite Owl
suspect
Karreem Washington
Ty Jones, Nite Owl suspect
Noel Evangelisti
stenographer
Marisol Padilla Sanchez
Inez Soto, rape victim
Jeff Sanders
Sylvester Fitch
Steve Lambert
Roland Navarette
Jordan Marder
officer at Detective Bureau
Gregory White
mayor
April Breneman
Lisa Worthy
lookalike dancers
Beverly Sharpe
witness on *Badge of Honor*
Colin Mitchell
reporter at hospital
John Slade
photographer at hospital
Brenda Bakke
Lana Turner
Kevin Maloney
Frolic Room bartender

Patrice Walters
Rebecca Jane Klingler
police file clerks
Irene Roseen
DA Ellis Loew's secretary
Scott Eberlein
West Hollywood sheriff's
deputy
David St James
detective at *Hush-Hush*
office
Bodie Newcomb
officer at *Hush-Hush* office
Jeff Austin
Robert Foster
Kevin Kelly
Henry Marder
Monty McKee
Henry Meyers
Michael Ossman
Dick Stilwell
Jess Thomas
Samuel Thompson
Jody Wood
Detectives

12,397 feet
137 minutes 45 seconds

Dolby
Colour by
Technicolor
2.35:1 [Super 35]

MPAA: 35218

**Filmed on location in Los
Angeles, California**

Credits compiled by Markku
Salmi, BFI Filmographic
Unit

Bibliography

Particularly valuable in writing this book were my interviews with James Ellroy (18 March 2002); Curtis Hanson (27 August 1997; 22 May 2002; also, emails from 31 January and 2 February 2003); and Jeannine Oppewall (24 March 2002). Another useful resource was Vikram Jiyanti's 2001 documentary *James Ellroy's Feast of Death*. The remainder of the production information is from the clippings files at the Margaret Herrick Library, located in Beverly Hills. All of the film's dialogue was transcribed directly from the Warner's DVD.

Banham, Reyner, *Los Angeles: The Architecture of Four Ecologies* (Berkeley: University of California Press, 2001).

Borde, Ramond and Étienne Chaumeton, 'Towards a Definition of *Film Noir*', in *Film Noir Reader* (New York: Limelight Editions, 1996).

Bowser, Eileen, *The Transformation of Cinema 1907–1915* (Berkeley: University of California Press, 1990).

Cain, James M., *The Postman Always Rings Twice* (New York: Vintage Books, 1978).

Caughey, John and LaRee (eds), *Los Angeles: Biography of a City* (Berkeley: University of California Press, 1977).

Chandler, Raymond, *The Big Sleep* (New York: Vintage Crime/Black Lizard, 1992).

——, *Raymond Chandler: Later Novels and Other Writings* (New York: The Library of America, 1995).

Domanick, Joe, *To Protect and To Serve: The LAPD's Century of War in the City of Dreams* (New York: Pocket Books, 1994).

Ellroy, James, 'Bad Boys in Tinseltown', in *Crime Wave: Reportage and Fiction from the Underside of L.A.* (London: Arrow Books, 1999), pp. 261–9.

——, *The Big Nowhere* (New York: The Mysterious Press, 1988).

——, *The Black Dahlia* (New York: The Mysterious Press, 1987).

——, *L.A. Confidential* (New York: The Mysterious Press, 1990).

——, *My Dark Places* (New York: Vintage Books, 1997).

——, *White Jazz* (New York: Fawcett Gold Medal, 1992).

Fante, John, *Ask the Dust* (Santa Rosa, CA: Black Sparrow Press, 1996).

Ferguson, Otis, *The Film Criticism of Otis Ferguson* (Philadelphia: Temple University Press, 1971).

Fine, Richard, *West of Eden: Writers in Hollywood 1928–1940* (Washington: Smithsonian Institution Press, 1993).

Fitzgerald, F. Scott, *The Love of the Last Tycoon* (New York: Scribner Paperback Fiction, 1994).

Frank, Robert, *The Americans* (New York: Pantheon Books, 1986).

Gabler, Neal, *Winchell: Gossip, Power and the Culture of Celebrity* (New York: Alfred A. Knopf, 1994).

Gilmore, John, *Severed: The True Story of the Black Dahlia Murder* (Los Angeles: Zanja Press, 1994).

Hammett, Dashiell, *Hammett: Crime Stories and Other Writings* (New York: The Library of America, 2001).

Hayde, Michael J., *My Name's Friday: The Unauthorized but True Story of Dragnet and the Films of Jack Webb* (Nashville, TN: Cumberland House, 2001).

Hecht, Ben, *A Child of the Century* (New York: Primus, 1985).

Helgeland, Brian and Curtis Hanson, *L.A. Confidential: The Screenplay* (New York: Warner Books, 1997).

Himes, Chester, *If He Hollers Let Him Go* (New York: Thunder's Mouth Press, 1986).

McWilliams, Carey, *Southern California: An Island on the Land* (Salt Lake City, UT: Peregrine Smith Books, 1995).

Orwell, George, *Down and Out in Paris and London* (New York: Harcourt Brace Jovanovich, 1961).

Rudolph, Eric, 'Exposing Hollywood's Sordid Past', *American Cinematographer*, October 1997, pp. 46–TK.

Sallis, James, *Chester Himes: A Life* (New York: Walker & Company, 2000).

Schulberg, Budd, *Moving Pictures: Memoirs of a Hollywood Prince* (London: Allison & Busby, 1993).

Skolnick, Jerome H. and James J. Fyfe, *Above the Law: Police and the Excessive Use of Force* (New York: The Free Press, 1994).

Slotkin, Richard, *Regeneration Through Violence: The Mythology of the American Frontier, 1600–1860* (Middletown, CT: Wesleyan University Press, 1973).

Szarkowski, John, *Photography Until Now* (New York: The Museum of Modern Art, 1989).

Todorov, Tzvetan, *The Poetics of Prose* (Ithaca, NY: Cornell University Press, 1984).

Torrence, Bruce, *Hollywood: The First 100 Years* (Hollywood, CA: The Hollywood Chamber of Commerce, 1979).

Walls, Jeannette, *Dish: The Inside Story on the World of Gossip* (New York: Avon Books, 2000).

Webb, Jack, *The Badge* (Greenwich, CT: Crest Book, 1959).

West, Nathanael, *Miss Lonelyhearts & The Day of the Locust* (New York: New Directions Paperbacks, 1969).

Wilson, Edmund, 'Who Cares Who Killed Roger Ackroyd?', in *Mass Culture: The Popular Arts in America* (New York: The Free Press, 1964).

Also Published

L'Argent
Kent Jones (1999)

Blade Runner
Scott Bukatman (1997)

Blue Velvet
Michael Atkinson (1997)

Caravaggio
Leo Bersani & Ulysse Dutoit (1999)

A City of Sadness
Bérénice Reynaud (2002)

Crash
Iain Sinclair (1999)

The Crying Game
Jane Giles (1997)

Dead Man
Jonathan Rosenbaum (2000)

Dilwale Dulhaniya Le Jayenge
Anupama Chopra (2002)

Don't Look Now
Mark Sanderson (1996)

Do the Right Thing
Ed Guerrero (2001)

Easy Rider
Lee Hill (1996)

The Exorcist
Mark Kermode (1997, 2nd edn 1998)

Eyes Wide Shut
Michel Chion (2002)

Heat
Nick James (2002)

Independence Day
Michael Rogin (1998)

Jaws
Antonia Quirke (2002)

Last Tango in Paris
David Thompson (1998)

Once Upon a Time in America
Adrian Martin (1998)

Pulp Fiction
Dana Polan (2000)

The Right Stuff
Tom Charity (1997)

Saló or The 120 Days of Sodom
Gary Indiana (2000)

Seven
Richard Dyer (1999)

The Silence of the Lambs
Yvonne Tasker (2002)

The Terminator
Sean French (1996)

Thelma & Louise
Marita Sturken (2000)

The Thing
Anne Billson (1997)

The 'Three Colours' Trilogy
Geoff Andrew (1998)

Titanic
David M. Lubin (1999)

Trainspotting
Murray Smith (2002)

The Usual Suspects
Ernest Larsen (2002)

The Wings of the Dove
Robin Wood (1999)

Women on the Verge of a Nervous Breakdown
Peter William Evans (1996)

WR – Mysteries of the Organism
Raymond Durgnat (1999)

BFI Modern Classics combine careful research with high-quality writing about contemporary cinema.

If you would like to receive further information about future **BFI Modern Classics** or about other books from BFI Publishing, please fill in your name and address and return this card to us.*

(No stamp required if posted in the UK, Channel Islands, or Isle of Man.)

NAME

ADDRESS

POSTCODE

WHICH BFI MODERN CLASSIC DID YOU BUY?

* In USA and Canada, please return your card to:
University of California Press, 2120 Berkeley Way,
Berkeley, CA 94720 USA

BFI Publishing
21 Stephen Street
FREEPOST 7
LONDON
W1E 4AN